Love-Pain Economics

by Rolf A. F. Witzsche

Contents

A story of the Kaleidoscope Project

It has been said that real economics begins with love expressed in the Principle of the General Welfare as the foundational economic principle. To the degree to which it is developed, civilization prospers, or is lost and, inversely, disintegrates. But what is love, to have this effect?

The story deals with the question in a Kaleidoscopic fashion that offers surprising new vistas at every turn. The story is situated in Leipzig, Germany. The protagonist is an American diplomat, who rather than being in control of things finds himself bewildered by the course of a love affair that unfolded more brilliantly than he has dared to hope for, but ended with a somewhat 'empty' tone. Here the world-critical story of economics begins that he knows nothing about, and much less has experienced. The story may be classified as social science fiction, but it really belongs into a class of its own for which no classification yet exists. It begins in the setting of a pub where many a question about love has been pondered over the centuries, and perhaps so even in political contexts.

The cover image for the book is of historic political significance, perhaps even of world-historic significance. Behind the entrance shown, to a small pub on a small street, a private meeting had taken place, as I was told recently, between Mikhail Gorbachev and a high-level official of the DDR government, perhaps with party chief Eric Honecker during the celebration of the 40th anniversary of the Republic in October 1989. No one knows what love 'pains' may have driven the agenda, as both had likely seen the writing on the wall, that without love for the general welfare, economies disintegrate, and that without economies, political regimes cannot stand. On November 9, that year, the Berlin Wall was breached that had imprisoned the nation. On December 1, the state essentially voted itself out of existence. A year and a half later, on December 25, 1991, then as President of the Soviet Union, Mikhail Gorbachev resigned. For all practical purposes, right of wrong, the Soviet Union had lost the heart of the people. Gorbachev resigned from an 'empty' seat.

The economics story in this book was not written with the political collapse in the East in mind. The story is situated a long time earlier when it appeared that the Communist regime would last a thousand years. The story was created to explore the economic principles, especially their root in love, and their reflection in civilization; and how the much-more devastating economic collapse of the West might be avoided by these principles.

The Kaleidoscope Project became a subsequent feature for me. I had started to write books that I would love, that are filled with a kaleidoscope of superlatives that define the riches of our humanity. My writing project began with two small novels, Flight Without Limits - a science fiction experiment to open the portal to the human superlatives - and a larger novel, Brighter than the Sun - a fictional project to explore the human dimension of the greatest intentional catastrophe that humanity has prepared against itself, termed "thermonuclear war" that is still on the agenda.

The larger novel explores against the background of catastrophe, the superlatives of the inner and enduring riches of our humanity. But the work didn't stop there. It just began. It became apparent that the human superlatives are so rich that they are best explored simply by themselves, for their own merit, so that a super-imposed context would tend to dilute them. The result became a series of twelve novels that I have named, The Lodging for the Rose. The work became a kaleidoscope-experience of superlatives, where new vistas of our inner riches come into view with every turn. The story in this book, is from Book 1 of the series.

As one might expect, many of the vistas are precious in themselves, so that it soon became apparent that quite a number of them stand on their own as complete stories and are important to raise up a specific focus that is of critical importance. I cherish these stories. Consequently, I started to share them in different forms, including now in printed form. The separate printing also allows a larger type face to be used.

The series *The Lodging for the Rose* - is published by Cygni Communications Ltd, BC, Canada (www.ice-age-ahead-iaa.ca)

The Kaleidoscope Project is also a part of the project: *Cool Science for Kids to have a Future in an Ice Age World*. The project can be found under topic #3, *Culture: The Science of Universal Love..*

Chapter 1 – Love Pains

The streets appeared much darker now, colder, and lifeless. The lanterns along the sidewalks shone faintly in the veil of mist that had drifted in from the nearby park, contrasting barely against the gray outline of the stone facades of buildings that lined the street. Equally faint was the noise of the city in the fog, compared to the grinding of my shoes on the sidewalk. The stillness though, wasn't productive. No answers emerged to the questions that I felt too impotent to even ask. The only sign of 'civilization' that called me to attention in this lonely silence, was the sour stench of another pub. I passed it by, but then stopped and went back. The smell was vented to the outside by a single small fan in the wall next to a window. I looked through the window. Only a few people could be seen inside. Normally this kind of heavy smell would have caused a sense of revulsion, but now it seemed inviting. There were people there, like me. It seemed natural to join them, to sit down with a beer, or two, and watch the world fade from view.

By the time the beer was delivered, and most of it was gulped down as if I wanted to drown myself in it, I noticed an elderly man on a stool not far from me. He had just received a fresh beer. He smiled and motioned me to join him. He, too, was alone.

He nodded slightly, as I joined him. "Love pains bring you here, no doubt," he said quietly, and put his beer down and looked at me as if he could find an answer in my expression, or by analyzing my clothing.

I nodded back. "Yes, and much more," I answered. I didn't care whether or not he understood what I meant.

"Most people who come here at this hour have love pains," he said. "They come here when they cannot sleep." He turned his barstool a bit more into my direction as he spoke. "Do you want to talk about it? Talking about it helps, you know."

I shook my head. Everything that troubled me was ultimately intertwined with the mission, and that was classified. "I feel I am being abused," I said quietly, just to say something. That much I could reveal. "I think I can understand what women must go through when they're being abused. It creates a deep gulf between people."

"I understand," the man answered. "Most people are reluctant to talk about specifics when they first come here, but let me tell you, most of the problems I have heard about are artificial. In fact, I haven't heard about any that aren't."

"Eh, you must be a psychiatrist," I replied in a somewhat cynical tone, and then emptied the last dregs of beer that were left.

He shrugged. "No, I am a professor of literature and history," he replied in a proud tone of voice. "I've been retired. I can tell you things about the real world that no psychiatrist knows. I can tell you about the separation of the sexes, and the separation of the world. Those two have caused all the wars in history." He paused. "The separation has been artificially created by people pursuing selfish purposes," he continued. "You can rely on that. I may not be a genius, as you probably surmise, but this one thing I know, and this, my friend, is already too much for anyone to hear."

"What are you saying?" I asked.

He shook his head slightly. "I cannot tell you more. If you knew what I know, it would kill you, just as it is killing me."

"Does this mean you have big problems at home that you don't want anyone to know about?" I said, probing.

A great burst of laughter was his response. "This place IS my home. I live here. Here I do not need to lye to myself. The biggest mistake I've ever made, my friend, was to study literature and history."

"So what?" I replied. "Many people study history and literature."

The man put his beer down. "Yes, they do. They read the textbooks and study lies. They don't study the literature that lays bare a poet's soul. When I studied Schiller, I knew I also had to study history in order to understand Schiller, because that man was deeply aware of the universal history of mankind. The two are one. And this, my friend, is the reason why I am here."

"History?" I repeated. I must have stared at him, perplexed by the paradox of a professor of history clutching his beer mug in this stinking hole in the wall, at one o'clock in the morning.

"Ah, I have you puzzled," he said smiling. He spoke English now. He spoke it well. He must have noticed my accent. "You are American, aren't you?"

I nodded cautiously. "I'm not here as an enemy. I'm on a diplomatic mission."

"Of course you are an enemy, a bigger enemy that you can imagine." He raised his beer mug. "You are a traitor to your country and an enemy to all mankind." He raised his mug higher. "Didn't I tell you that you don't want to hear what I know?" He raised his mug higher still. "Here is one for you!" he said and lowered the mug again, and turned to the bar tender, saying in German, "bring my brother another beer."

"Are you American, too?" I asked.

"No I am not!" he said proudly. "But we are both fellow traitors. We are both fighting on the wrong side in the war of empire versus civilization."

"The war of empire versus civilization?" I repeated. "We are not at war. World War II has ended decades ago."

"Yes it has," he said and smiled, as if speaking to a child. "But the real war that threads through all history, the war of empire versus civilization, has never ended. It began in ancient times and has been maintained by every empire that ever was. Plato understood this. The war of empire versus civilization had destroyed the Greek Classical Culture. Athens has had its own Thirty Years War, by which it lost everything. Plato discovered that the war of empire versus civilization is designed to diminish the human being, to make the human being small, weak, dumb, and easily defeasible, so that society will never become a threat to empire. Understanding this, Plato struggled to bring the lost Greek culture back, by promoting a profound recognition of the greatness of the human being. Some call him the precursor to the unfolding of Christianity. He was a great man, but the war of empire versus civilization continued. After Persia destroyed itself with its madness, Rome carried the torch of empire and proceeded to burn down civilization. It nearly succeeded in destroying it, before it destroyed itself. Islam rose out of the ashes, and brought the dignity of the human being back into view. With it, it brought back the development of science, and of course Plato. Plato in turn rescued Europe when the war of the Lombard banking empire versus civilization had created a disaster in the 14th Century that had wiped out half the population. The revival of Plato by the Islamic Renaissance, brought the perception of the value of the human being back to Europe, and set the stage for the Golden Renaissance. The Renaissance nearly succeeded in closing the door to empire, possibly forever, but the Pope intervened and kept the door open. The Venetian Empire survived and started a subversive religious war to destroy the Renaissance that had threatened its existence. It took more than a hundred years to destroy the Renaissance completely. The devastation was so great that Europe lost a third of its population, especially in the latter part of it, in the Thirty Years War. But a spark of the Renaissance Spirit survived. It was brought back to the foreground where it caused a renewed recognition of the value of the human being. Out of it came the greatest peace treaty in history, the Treaty of Westphalia. While the Peace of Westphalia didn't last, the little renaissance that had created it, gave rise to the founding of the USA as a Plato-type republic in which the human being was recognized as of great value. The USA became the guiding star of the world, and the hope of mankind. It was the most daring large-scale breakout ever attempted by society, from the rule of empire. By this it posed the most serious threat to the existence of empire itself. Thus the war of empire versus civilization was put into high gear, in order to destroy the USA, and to also destroy all the intellectual elements in Europe that had stood behind the American republic and had helped bring it about. The empire's French Revolution, the war of empire that Napoleon rose from, accomplished the desired intellectual destruction all across France, and then across Europe. While Napoleon failed in his biggest task, to take Russia down, the empire succeeded through the back door. The empire created communism as a Trojan horse that succeeded subversively in what Napoleon had been unable to do with force. But the biggest thrust in the war of empire versus civilization has always been directed against America, as the chief threat to empire. The empire failed on the battlefield to recapture America, it also failed on the high sees to defeat America there, but it nearly succeeded in destroying America by way of a civil war. Still it failed. It failed on all of these fronts, until it eventually succeeded subversively. This happened on the day before Christmas in 1913.On this day America was destroyed by traitors, traitors like you my friend. America betrayed the whole of mankind." The man raised his beer mug and smiled, waiting for a response.

"I'm not a traitor," I said, raising my hands with a gesture of protest.

"Oh yes you are a traitor to your country, and the thereby the enemy of mankind," he said and almost grinned. "And I can proof it to you?" he added.

I took my beer that the bar tender had brought. "This is going to be interesting," I said.

The man shook his head. "That's easy! Can you name the one fundamental difference that set the USA apart from any other nation on the planet, when it was founded? And I mean something as distinctly different as black and white, and something so profound that it became known in many parts of the world as the American system. I bet you can't tell me what this is." The man raised his mug. "I think I got you on this one," he added with a smile.

I looked down onto my beer mug as if an answer could be found there. "What do you mean with, the American System? In today's world America is the world leader in many types of systems."

"Your ignorance proves that you are a traitor," said the man and smiled. "There are two types of economic systems in the world. Both are central to the war of empire versus civilization. There is the monetarist system of empire that every empire must defend as it is the very core of its existence. The monetarist system is a liberal system of private money estates. The system is the bastion of the modern empire's liberal, unrestrained power to loot. Everyone who has the power to do so is free to reap profit by any means possible. It's done on a similar basis as the landed feudalism once functioned. Liberal monetarism is essentially a private system of looting. It is a private method of stealing from society in clever schemes. The process expresses the dictum of empire that aims to diminish the value of the human being. It causes society to put value on money, while this process takes more than the equivalent in value away from humanity itself. It says that human productivity has little value. It says that only money invested for making money makes society rich. So be greedy, it says, and speculate. Of course the empire runs all the 'casinos' and only the empire gets rich in the process, flush with stolen loot, while society foots the bill, and becomes poor and diminished, though it is actually the creator of all the real wealth there is. The whole monetarist system is built on a lye that enables the looting of society. The American system is the opposite. It is not a system of private banks and private money estates. It is a system of banks owned by the nation for the benefit of the nation. Thus the national bank utters financial credits specifically directed to such enterprises that improve the general welfare, like productive industries, national infrastructures such as railways and power systems. Here the wealth that is produced by the productive processes that improve the living of society and uplift civilization, gives a nation's currency its value. That's the American system of economy. It is a focused credit system that functions specifically to improve the general welfare. That's the American System of Political Economy. It doesn't diminish the human being, but develops the value that is inherent in our common humanity. On this platform the USA stood as a pioneer for all of humanity. Of course you wouldn't know anything about that, because this system was destroyed on the day before Christmas in 1913, long before you were born, and was replaced on this day with the old private monetarist system of empire. The old private monetarist system of empire is obviously the only system that you ever knew. And that is why I must call you a traitor," said the man and raised his beer mug again.

I shook my head. "You are crazy," I said to him. "How can you accuse me of something that happened long before I was born?"

"You are a traitor, because you didn't make it your business to discover what your country represents. It was the hope of mankind. It gave value to the human being. It raised the general welfare. It defended mankind in the war of empire versus civilization. It was the light on the hill that mankind looked up to. But America gave all that away. It intentionally joined the empire, by accepting the rule of private imperial monetarism in America. America became a traitor against its own birthright. It literally joined the enemy of mankind. Is it any wonder then that World War I broke out less than a year later? You are a traitor to your country, my friend, by not fighting for your country's birthright, and by quietly abetting the enemy of mankind that diminishes the value of the human being, and is now evermore demanding the mass-depopulation of the planet. If that doesn't make you a traitor, what would? With traitors like you in the world, what hope is there left for mankind? What hope does anyone have?"

I shook my head again in disbelief. He was right. I didn't want to hear this.

"In order for you Americans to understand anything at all about the history of humanity and the world around you, you have to recognize that there are two opposing forces in the world that have been at war with each other for the last six hundred years," said the man. "Before that time the war of empire versus civilization was virtually unopposed. But will you ever discover that you are right in the middle of that war, and oppose it once again, before it destroys America totally?"

He explained that "the war of empire versus civilization" as he called it, is rooted in the oligarchic, feudal tradition that maintains a privately directed system of government, which enables the rich to steal their opulent living from the labors of humanity. "They do it by clever games and special privileges," he said.

13

"The other force that I spoke of," he said, "the one opposing them, is the republican spirit of humanity, which promotes the self-development of individuals and nations. The founding of America was mankind's proudest achievement on this front. Before it was destroyed, the American System had uplifted all of Europe, especially Germany. The great Bismarck reforms that had built-up Germany and had put it on the map of progress, had been an expression of your achievements. But who remembers any of it? Who is fighting to bring sanity back? And that makes me a traitor too, because I don't know how to fight to get the kind of Germany back that had reflected your republican ideals of uplifting the value of the human being. We got Hitler instead, another Trojan Horse uttered in the war of empire versus civilization."

The man said that the greatest development period in history was the Golden Renaissance. Its focus was on the dignity of man, and on the common welfare of society. He went on to say that the unfolding new perception had been so immense at first that the powers of the Renaissance had banded together to rid the world of the last major outpost of feudalism. This happened to be the Venetian Empire, the foremost slave trader of the Old World. The man said, that this quest by the Renaissance powers would surely have succeeded had the Venetian Empire not persuaded the Pope as the head of another empire, to intervene. His intervention saved the Venetian Empire from being wiped out. From this point on, the feudal powers have been at war with the powers of the Renaissance spirit. The Thirty Years War that devastated Europe, was the first major outcome of this confrontation, and so was every war that followed, including the first and second world wars. "Even communism was created as a part of the war of empire to defeat the Renaissance spirit, that is, to defeat the self-development of humanity."

The man tried to catch the attention of the bar tender while he spoke, but this didn't change his focus. "Carl Marx was not the creator of communism," he said to me. "Marx was a willing student who was ideologically guided by a man named David Urquhard, a British Aristocrat and specialist in the art of psychological warfare, under the direction of Lord Palmerston set up by the second Earl of Shelburne. This means that communism was the concoction of the aristocrats. The script was written in London. The project was directed from the highest levels of the British Empire. Now I want to hear you tell me that this game was invented to elevate humanity. The goal was to destroy the industrial machine of continental Europe and Russia, which had become powerful, and had thereby become a threat to the British Empire."

The man had emptied his glass before the bar tender came by again, then ordered another one, though he didn't drink of it. He explained that a feudal empire exists entirely from the proceeds of looting. "It's been like that throughout all history," he said. "In order to maintain itself in power, a feudal empire must create poverty. Poverty prevents the rise of a resistance to its rule. The empire has no choice in the matter. Unfortunately for us, the last surviving feudal empire has become a near global empire that is determined to create and maintain poverty on a global scale. History teaches us that a feudal empire has no option, but to do this. History also teaches us that the best way to create large-scale poverty is to cause wars, especially ideological wars, and internally subversive wars that destroy industries and populations. Of course, in our modern world, the feudal powers conduct these wars mainly financially, and in a hidden way, ideologically arranged, in order to instigate division and universal chaos."

The man started to drink his beer now, but soon he put it down again. He brought a tattered paperback book out of his coat pocket. He opened the book up and began to read it and then closed it again. "That's why the British Empire has been such a vocal advocate for world-depopulation, and still is," he said, "by whatever means this can be achieved. It's part of the war of empire versus civilization."

He put the book down and muttered something about "the damn royals who think they own the whole world." His hands were shaking. Then he muttered something about a prince who wants to be reincarnated as a particularly deadly virus in order that he may contribute to the world-population reduction. "Can you see the connection?" the man asked. "The prince uses this ploy to achieve by means of mass murder what he knows his empire must achieve to maintain its power. In real terms the world isn't too full by any means. In comparison to what is required for humanity's proper self-development, our world is dramatically under-populated. There aren't enough people in the world to fulfill the human mission, to prepare this planet for the next Ice Age. We are the eighth human species. The seven other species have all become extinct, probably in one of the many ice ages."

It was hard to make out precisely what he was saying. Was he seriously speaking of another Ice Age hitting this planet, or was he just 'dreaming?' The night wasn't young by any means. According to the evidence, he had been at this pub for quite some time.

While holding the beer mug in both of his hands, carefully, as though it was a holy object, he nodded to me. "Do you know what they refer to as over-population?" He paused, and took another sip, as though he needed it to be able to announce the answer. "They mean that two thirds of humanity must be culled like a bloated heard of cattle." He spoke angrily now. No longer mentioning the Ice Age. His words were carefully spoken, so that there would be no misunderstanding about the scale of the promoted genocide. "It won't come to that," he added. "The Soviet Union will fall," he said, as if this explained it all. I looked at him perplexed. He had obviously one too many.

"The Soviet Union can't survive the arms race against the whole world," he said moments later. He pulled himself together and spoke clearly now. "The arms race will destroy the Soviet economy," he said. "Then the empire's royals will come in with an olive branch in hand, while their sharks will loot Russia through the back door to the point that many millions of people can no longer maintain their existence. Russia is not excluded from the war of empire versus civilization, my friend. The goal of empire is, and always has been, to destroy any competition. Therefore, the policy targets Russia and its population. This particular goal has been pursued for two hundred years already. At the present stage in the war of empire versus civilization, they will do it. There is nothing that can be done to stop them." The man put his mug down and sighed.

The old professor now spoke about Schiller again. He asked whether I read Schiller. He said that Schiller was right when he lamented that all the great moments in history, at which deep reaching changes could have

16

been wrought, found humanity a small-minded people so that in the end nothing was done. "That is how Hitler was able to grab power, richly financed from England and America," he added, "and that's also why the world is now poised to go to hell." He said that all of Europe should band together when the Soviet Union falls. They should develop Europe, Russia and Asia into one single, modern, efficient economy, so that there will be peace at last, but it won't happen. Mark my word, it won't happen. And that is why the world is domed. If we were to stand together, all of us, all nations, determined to put an end to the war of empire against civilization, and redevelop the world with real economics, unfolding in real sovereign nations, then we might have a chance. Otherwise doom awaits mankind. In the wake of this doom no nation will survive when the next Ice Age transition begins, and our agriculture fails. We have wasted fifty centuries being strangled in this war of empire versus civilization, by which progress had been reduced to a snail's pace. We might only have two centuries left, my friend, or one, if that. Don't even think about global warming, that's the deadliest political farce ever unleashed in the war of empire versus civilization. The return of the Ice Age is real. Galactic clockworks run its schedule. We know that ice age cycles have hit us for the last two million years in roughly 100,000 year-intervals without fail. The next one is now before us. Standing together as human beings we can survive that threat, but we won't with the war of empire constantly killing us, bit by bit."

"Why then don't we stand together as one and end the war of empire against us?" I interjected.

"Because America is a nation of traitors, as I pointed out before," said the man. "We are all traitors on that count, and enemies of mankind, and thereby enemies of ourselves. First, we have to learn to stop being traitors."

He reached for his glass again and emptied it to the last drop, then pointed to the clock and said that it was time to go. He said he was tired enough now, to sleep.

Before he stood up I was able to ask him, how any of this could possibly be related to love pains, as he had suggested in the beginning.

"That is for you to figure out," he said slowly, and began to grin. He wasn't too steady on his feet. "For this you have to go much farther back into history," he added, and tapped his fingers on my shoulder as he stood beside me. "If I was you, I wouldn't concern myself with it," he reversed himself. "Concern yourself with the real world." He emphasized, "real." "Respond to it honestly," he added. "Stop being a traitor. Maybe people will respect you for the gesture. They certainly don't respect you if you tell them the truth. That's why I am not teaching anymore. That's why I am here in this hellhole. Our society has become a society of liars as well as traitors. People lye to their governments, they lye to each other, to their friends, to their spouses, but most of all they lye to themselves. And this, my friend, is destroying your chance to free yourself from being a traitor. Think about that. "In Lies We Trust!" This is the modern watchword. One of the biggest lies in modern times is the lye you Americans believe in, that you live in an era of prosperity. The fact is, that the entire world-economy has collapsed to half of what it used to be. It was once possible for a single worker to buy a house and support a family of three. This was possible once in America, a few decades ago. I have read that it now takes three people working full time, to accomplish the same, if they are lucky enough to get the jobs. This leaves not a single person of the family left over to look after the children. That isn't prosperity, it is insanity. Our world is doomed by insanity."

Chapter 2 – Empty Riches

The man then laughed and put both his hands on my shoulders, as though he would shake me to my senses. He said that people lye to themselves when they believe that their laboriously accumulated financial portfolios represent riches. "There exists no real wealth anywhere apart from that which society creates for itself," he said, "no matter how much the people's financial portfolios hold."

He took hold of my beer mug. He said its content represents the total product of society. He said that it doesn't really matter how much money society has in its portfolios, it cannot buy more than what is in its mug, because that's all what is being produced. Whether society has a trillion, or ten trillion, or a thousand trillion in financial wealth, it can't buy anything more than what is being produced. He pointed to my beer mug. The mug was almost empty.

"It is stupidity for society to imagine that its financial wealth can buy more than what is being produced," he added. "But that's what people believe they can do. They have become enslaved to empire. They accumulate financial wealth, and destroy by this process the foundation for the economy that alone produces things of value. They are traitors to themselves. They have joined the war of empire versus civilization on the side of empire, fighting against their own welfare and existence."

He pointed out that over the last several decades the financial values have increased twenty-fold, especially in America, while at the same time the economic output has collapsed to half of what it was. He took a large sip from my mug, and pointed out that it is now empty. "That's all what their trillions of money can buy," he said.

I shook my head in disbelief.

"Don't blame me," he said. "Blame the ancient Egyptians. Blame the Pharaohs. They started the insanity of building empires on slavery. To be able to do this they prevented the development of love in sexual intimacies. They sexually mutilated their slaves in order to take that away from them. They mutilated them to make them better slaves. They circumcised the men. They infibulated the women. The masters that the Pharaohs set over the slaves took away the very heart of what holds a society together. On this empty platform the masters of the slaves created one of the greatest slavery empires. But it was precisely this success that destroyed Egypt. The slavery process eventually destroyed all the cultural advances that the ancient Egyptians had developed. No my friend, Egypt wasn't built on slavery, as most people think. It was destroyed by it from within. It was collapsed by it. Now the world is following the same path. Almost a third of the entire male population of our planet is living as victims of the circumcision. Without even realizing it, the mutilated victims are swelling the ranks of the modern slaves in the service of empire. Nothing has changed, my friend, since the Pharaohs ruled, except perhaps the face of it. So you have come here with love pains. You are probably here, because of something that the Pharaohs had set in motion almost five millennia ago, that no one has so far dealt with, which has festered over time and grown worse. This means, my friend, that you are not alone. The whole world is presently caught in the same trap. The whole world should have love pains for reasons of what the Pharaohs had started. It would, if it hadn't become desensitized, as slaves do become. Nevertheless, what the Pharaohs have started is now destroying our world as surely as it once destroyed theirs from within, and I see no way to stop the outcome that will end civilization."

The man paused, then added quietly that this is the future of humanity and the we were getting close to the end of it. "Right now," he said, "the real value of the world's money is worth 50 times less than what it used to be in the mid sixties. The collapse is that fast and is accelerating. On this axis of poverty, everything is already in the process of collapsing. With the process escalating exponentially, the outcome will likely be open universal war, unless the process is reversed, and the war that results when the process is not reverse will be a nuclear war, because that is the only type of warfare that remains economically feasible in a physically collapsing world."

He then paused once more, and fumbled for something in his pockets. Eventually he gave up searching. "This is the truth," he said, "except you can't tell it to anyone. People want to hear lies. 'In Lies We Trust!' That's the motto. People want to hear that they are rich, even though the world is collapsing under their feet. Nothing is real anymore, my friend. What people believe in is artificial, even that which separates the sexes. Nobody believes anymore in what is real, including the riches mankind has in sex. Those are being shunned. We have become a society of perfect slaves, my friend. We certainly behave like slaves."

With this said, the man walked away. He turned around at the door and smiled with a wicked kind of look. "There, my friend, is your connection to the love pains. People have been lying to each other and to themselves for centuries. Why would this suddenly change? Why would people suddenly treat each other as human beings? Can you solve that paradox? You can't, can you? That is why love pains are good for the pubs. They will never run out of customers for that reason."

I remained at the bar after he was gone. The man seemed to know something about the deep things Erica and I had explored, though we had explored them in a different context. Nowhere in the world could I have listened to a more powerful lecture on this subject, than in this hole in the wall in the middle of the night. In the context of what Erica and I had explored all day in different ways, I knew the old professor was right in his perception of the present world. That meant that all the political lectures and lectures on economics and history that I had listened to before were totally built on fakery, distortions of fact, and possibly deliberate lies. Perplexed, I ordered another beer. I could see why the professor had called this hellhole his home. It had become a trap away from the real trap.

I didn't finish the beer. I barely drank any of it. I left it sitting on the counter and walked out.

On the way to the hotel I wished that I had never set foot in this damn, dark place, where my illusions about the world had been so cruelly overturned with his blunt exposition of what seemed to be the truth. The overturning of my perception of the world, included the scope of my mission. Yes, he had answered some of my questions that I had struggled to come to terms with, which I had tried to avoid in the hope of finding peace. I had been clinging to answers that provided comfortable illusions, rather than the nagging truth that was becoming evident everywhere. I also realized that I had found no peace in the pub on this ground, only more pain. Something had been spiritually missing. Strangely, I found myself being grateful for the rare opportunity that I had been given, to be confronted with all the darkness that was obviously the state of the world. For me, his blunt demand to face an ugly dimension, outweighed all the comforts that one imagines to derive from comfortable lies.

I promised myself to be more sensitive to the truth in the future, and to be more honest with myself. Except, I realized that this is more easily said than done. Perhaps, a person like myself with a shallow perception of things and with less honesty than the professor demanded, needs to go right back to the fundamentals and begin one's own research of the dimensions of love as Erica had found this necessary as a means for dealing with the larger dimension.

I hadn't gone more than a hundred yards, towards the hotel, when a woman called out to me. I glanced back. I saw her standing in front of the pub, waving. "Please wait," she called and started walking towards me, swiftly. When she arrived, she was quite out of breath.

"You didn't find in the pub what you were seeking," she said and reached her hand out. "Am I right? I can help you to find that," she added, still holding her hand out. "My name is Helen."

I introduced myself and said that I was a diplomat. I told her that I had actually found more in the pub than what I came for. "The professor explained a lot to me that I knew little about," I said. "Now I understand a great deal more. At least I understand something that I didn't understand before."

"Except Love," she added. "You don't understand what Love is. The professor is right; you came here because of love pains, but he couldn't answer you, because he doesn't know. So he told you all about the history of the world, at least what he knows about it. I overheard some of your conversation. I also think that what you talked about wasn't what you came to the pub for. I think that something went sour in your private loving, or it didn't go far enough, or it has you puzzled. That's why you came to the pub, right? You came to figure things out. Unfortunately, the professor couldn't help you. He couldn't, because he doesn't understand what Love is. I know this, because I tried to teach him. Eventually, I realized that the subject is too difficult for him."

"You taught the professor?"

"Not really. I taught him history. I tried to teach him the real history of humanity, not that which empire teaches, but real history. Empire twists history to project a humanity that is fractured and divided. It needs these distortions to promote its long-standing game of divide and conquer. Are you willing to learn a bit of the Truth that the professor knows nothing about?"

"I found the professor amazingly knowledgeable," I countered her.

"He appears that way, but appearances can be misleading if one lacks the necessary points of reference," she said. She began to smile.

I loved her smile. Her face sparkled as she spoke. "You say, empire twists history," I repeated.

She nodded quietly. "It aids their game of divide and conquer. But it also has much wider consequences. It divides us, sexually, you and me, and the whole of mankind, causing love pains."

"You say, for this goal of divide to conquer, the official concepts of history are twisted?" I said, to keep the conversation going. She intrigued me, suddenly. She was older than Erica, but just as exciting to look at.

"It is archeology that has been twisted under the control of the British Empire," she said. "It has been done for spreading the notion that the dawn of civilization has begun independently in the great river valleys of the world, like in Mesopotamia, the Nile Valley, or the Indus Valley, and produced fundamentally different races of people, and so forth. This is a gross distortion of history."

This wasn't the answer I had expected. Also the timing was odd. It was past midnight. Nevertheless, it seemed important to let her go on. I nodded.

"What the professor doesn't understand is simple," said Helen. "The dawn of civilization began along the seashores, because living is easier there, especially where the fish are plentiful. With the development of fishing, began the development of shipbuilding, and out of that flowed an amazing mobility for people. With discoveries of navigation, increasingly longer voyages became possible. As the result, the people began to intermingle, sometimes across large distances. In real terms the entirety of mankind is made up of one single people with the same innate human quality and the same capacity for reason. The settlements along the river valleys, and the development of agriculture, began much later in time. Mankind, the species called the homosapien, has been around for roughly 200,000 years, spreading and intermingling. In real terms the whole of mankind is one, like one universal family. Nothing fundamentally divides us. The division became superimposed when the periods of empire began. Agriculture, is only 10,000 years old, and empire far less than that. Mankind has been one people, reflecting a single fundamental humanity right across the planet. This happened long before the regional developments began. Nor did the regional developments change our native character as a people, and diminish our common humanity. The vast racial divisions that we now have in the world, and the religious divisions, and economic divisions, are all games built on lies. They are the lies of empire. Real history therefore comes to the foreground by putting the lies aside, by stepping away from the games of empire, and by recognizing ourselves as human beings, universally, undivided, unfettered. Love is deeply intertwined with that. It stands at the core of it. Are you interested to learn history?"

Chapter 3 – History and Love in the Middle of the Night

"History and Love, in the middle of the night?" I repeated. "Are you saying that Love threads through all history?"

" This is what I had tried to teach the professor," she said. "I felt he should know about that, if he wants to teach others. He understands some of it, but he doesn't understand enough of it to understand what Love is. Love is anchored in Truth. It begins with discovering aspects of Truth. In recent years I tried to get the professor to relive the discoveries of the great pioneers of humanity, especially in terms of the discovery of Love. I had many a long discussion with him on that point, however, it has become too much of a challenge for him, especially the discovery of Love. And so, he couldn't really answer your question, and help you with your love pain."

"The discovery of Love?" I repeated.

"We all need to replicate in our own mind the great discoveries that have come to light and have created our civilization," said Helen. "We need to get to the core of what the greatest pioneers of humanity have discovered in cultural and scientific terms to uplift one another and enrich each other's life, which can be summed up as the discovery of Love."

"Love is as ancient as the hills, Helen," I reminded her.

"That it is, but it wasn't put onto the map, formally for a very long time, actually not until the early 1400s. Are you willing to learn? If so, I'll present to you a world that the professor never understood, and probably never will. It may change your life."

Since her offer sounded intriguing, and she was already leading the way, I nodded, and simply continued on following her. Also I loved her voice and her exciting appearance as a woman.

But was she leading me into a trap? Was she a prostitute? "Don't do this! Don't follow her! You are a married man," I heard a voice say within me, urging me. The voice was quickly suppressed as if its warning was not applicable this time. I realized that if that kind of warning had occurred earlier, I might not have allowed myself to meet Erica at all. What a tragic loss that would have been in terms of the riches that we had shared? Nor had my being open and honest with Erica, and with myself, done any harm. "Why should there be any danger now?" I replied and hushed the voice.

"Don't be stupid. Go with her and embrace the wisdom that she may share," I heard another voice saying within, a quieter and gentler voice.

I told the woman that I felt deeply honored by her offer to help me. I loved the sound of her name, Helen. The name seemed related to hope. I hadn't actually accepted that the professor was totally right. Also she was correct about figuring me out. I had been struggling with love pains, trying to discover what had moved me so deeply. That exploration had been interrupted with politics, because the professor didn't know what else to talk about. She was right about that, too.

"Let me ask you one important question," Helen interrupted my pondering after a while of silence. "Why are you allowing me so freely to invite you? What would your wife say? I bet you are feeling deep in your heart that you shouldn't be here with me. Am I correct? So, why are you?"

"I think I should ask you that question first," I replied. "You should tell me why you are inviting me. Obviously you are not a prostitute. You are far too beautiful for that, and too well dressed, and too kindly mannered. Prostitutes don't stay like that for long. You say you want to teach me what Love is. You are inviting me into your home. If you want to talk about Love, the pub would have been fine. Of course you are right, that is what I came to the pub for. But why are you putting yourself at risk, inviting a strange man into your home in the middle of the night?"

She began to laugh, interrupting me. "I am not putting myself at risk. I think I can trust you, and you can trust me. I'm not trying to corrupt a foreign diplomat." She intertwined her arm with mine as we walked. "I watched you, and the professor. I watched your face, your reaction. You didn't quite believe the professor, but you listen to him. You listened to him out of respect. That's what I think. You listened to his entire story. I know his story by heart. Nor were you the first to leave, as other men might have out of disgust. The professor left first."

"So you feel the same way about that, that his story isn't totally true," I said. "It made sense to me to a point, Helen."

"Oh it's technically correct," she replied, "but too much is missing. There is no reference to Love in what he says. There is something spiritually lacking. I could sense that you understood this. I could sense your sadness." She laughed. "But now it is your turn to answer me," she said. "Why are you following me so freely? Why do you allow yourself to follow me and put yourself at risk with your wife? Is it really love-pains?"

I nodded. "The answer is both yes and no. There shouldn't be any love pain," I replied. "I have been all day with a most wonderful woman. I met her at the Kolkwitzer-Lake beach. We had dinner together. We had danced. We also had the deepest reaching conversations. In the end, however, she couldn't bring herself to take that final step in being close to each other. She barely allowed me to drive her home. We never touched each other sexually. She is afraid that we might. You are right. Marriage is at the center of this impasse. That's why she won't allow me to meet her again. She is afraid that going further might hurt her husband. That's the very thing that puzzled you about me. And to be honest, I am glad for the same reason, that she drew that line in the sand. I also think she really wanted to take that next step. So did I. She spoke about living our life as being in a flower garden with a vast profusion of beautiful shapes, colors, and fragrance all around us. She evidently also sees herself forcefully isolated, almost forced to look at just one of the flowers in the garden of life, as if life needs to be narrow, confined, without the liberty to love fully. I think my love pain is more her pain. Can you understand what I am saying? Do I make sense?"

Helen stopped and kissed me briefly, as if to make up for that pain, and she did so with the most wonderful smile that seemed brighter than Erica's had been. "Your friend is as wrong about her flower garden, as the professor is about politics," said Helen while we continued walking. "However, I didn't ask you about your friend. I asked you about yourself. Why do you allow yourself to follow me? Isn't there some inkling deep in your heart, telling you that what you're doing is wrong?"

I nodded. "I think this inkling is wrong," I said quietly. "I think what I am doing is right."

"Why Peter? Why is it right?"

I didn't know how to answer that. "Why shouldn't it be right?" I said in a small tone of voice. "You are a human being as much as I am. You look the same, except you're more beautiful than I. You speak the same language. You have the same wonderful human concerns, the same feelings as a person, and the same intelligence that I admire, which makes us both rather special as human beings. Why shouldn't I embrace that? Also you talk about Love, a subject that is dear to my heart. The fact is, Helen, it appears to me now that you make me look deep into myself. You force me to acknowledge that we are more deeply and profoundly married to each other by what unites us on this platform of truth, than by the marriage division that would isolate us. Why should I not respond to such a beautiful human invitation, as you have extended? We are not enemies, you and I. Just look at us. We could be brothers and sisters. Actually we are this, and in a more truthful sense than people are who regard themselves merely biologically related. So why shouldn't I respond to my sister when she offers to share a few insights about the nature of Love? I think what you are offering is the most natural thing in the world. Nevertheless, the voice within keeps nagging, saying this is wrong. To hell with this chattering! What I am doing is right. The truth is the truth. We are two human beings, and I admire you in this context. That is the truth. Maybe that is where loving begins, Helen. Anyway, does that answer your question?"

She didn't answer, as if no answer was needed. The air didn't feel as cold anymore as we walked, and the streets, as eerily empty. "My friend's name is Erica. She is studying Love," I added moments later before Helen could answer my question.

"But your friend doesn't understand what Love is," Helen replied. "She doesn't understand it, according to the way that you have just described your affair with her. I think, that is why she can't acknowledge that she is in Love. I sense, that you have the same problem. I sense a conflict in you. In fact, you said so yourself. You are scared to accept the truth that you know to be true. You are scared that you will hurt your wife, if you come with me to my apartment. On the other hand, you are also afraid that you will hurt yourself, by denying yourself the chance to explore what you have closed your mind to for almost your entire life, which is a truth that you have always known, and never allowed yourself to acknowledge. But why should there be a conflict? Most people that I know struggle with this conflict, and are actually afraid to resolve it. Just look at yourself, you are a married man for a dozen years or more. But let me ask you this: When you put on that ring, did you stop being a human being with human feelings and a need to respond to these feelings? When you put on that ring, did you swear to isolate yourself from your innermost humanity, that we all share, by which we are all united, which draws us all together into a single, universal humanity? Did you swear to close the door on all that? Obviously you haven't. Still, you treat yourself as if you had. You treat yourself badly. You treat yourself like a criminal. In a way you are a criminal. You are denying yourself and me, and the whole of humanity, as human beings. That's a paradox, isn't it? I think your friend Erica doesn't understand a lot about that either, just like you. That is why you're both glad that you didn't get any closer. You couldn't move further. You were stuck. You didn't have a platform worked out, where Love can reign more freely. Of course, you are also both sad about it. You embraced each other as two equal human beings, and you were glad about it, but than you rejected the very thing that you embraced, which is your common humanity? Why couldn't you treat each other as brother and sister, as you really are in the most profound sense? I think, that is what your friend doesn't understand. Neither do you understand this."

I nodded, but then shook my head. "I think she understands a lot about Love," I said. "She has taught me a lot about myself."

"Except she fails to understand one thing," Helen interjected and shook her head slightly. "She has read the textbooks, Peter. She has studied love that is written in small letters. But in life, Love isn't a small thing. She said no, to life! She said no, no, no, to living in the realm of truth. She literally preferred clinging to a lye. That's not living, Peter, is it? So, what is missing, Peter? Tell me!"

I couldn't answer. I let us fall silent again. I hated that.

"You accepted a great responsibility with that ring," Helen continued, "and I am sure you're fulfilling it. But that shouldn't become so overbearing that it isolates you from the rest of humanity and from yourself, and builds a fence around you. To the contrary, you should see your marriage as but a first step towards embracing the universal marriage of the whole of mankind on the basis of our common humanity that we all share. It seems to me that you have been running backwards. You have been running away from Love, and from your responsibility to be loving in ever brighter ways. But running away from Love doesn't accord with the principle of life and of our humanity. Life isn't a catch-me-if-you can race, in which a person becomes another's trophy. Life is wide, profound, beautiful, rich and exciting, and it will be that if you allow it to unfold. We've got to become responsive to its principles, Peter. Every lye hurts us. A lye is corrosive. Embracing the truth, to as far as you can see it, brings stability and substance to living."

Helen paused and sighed. "Why couldn't you and Erica do that? What principle that you know as a truth, didn't you understand, Peter, so that you got stuck?"

"I think Erica was afraid of committing adultery," I replied, just to say something. "She still is. I think she would have loved to embrace living and loving more fully, even as fully as possible, but she couldn't, and still can't. In a way we are all a bit like that. It seems to me, that Erica doesn't own herself. She doesn't respect her sovereignty as a human being. If she did,

31

she wouldn't have hesitated to allow us to embrace one-another fully, to the fullest extend that our loving would have urged us to go."

"Would you have respected her sovereignty?" Helen replied. This time she didn't smile. "Would you have allowed anything to happen between you that you would ever have to be ashamed about, both she and you, as two human beings bound in a bond of Love? But before you answer, forget about marriage. Too many married people do things to each other that a human being should never do to another person. Many ugly things seem to be allowed in marriage. Especially a lot of cruel things are allowed in marriage. People tare each other down, instead of aiding each other in building up their self-esteem. I think this tearing down happens especially in marriage, because the currently narrow marriage institution literally prevents the development of Love. It makes people enemies of one-another. It shuts down the process of embracing one-another on the basis of what is really true. That's sad, isn't it? So, Peter, I am offering you a chance to breathe freely again as a human being. I am offering you a chance to discover Love, not to learn about it. But isn't this what you really had hoped to accomplish in your association with Erica? Be honest about it."

I nodded slightly.

"Would there have been any danger involved for her, or you, if you had allowed yourself to accomplish that?" said Helen. "I want an unbiased honest answer that comes from the heart," she added moments later. "Would you have respected her sovereignty? Would anything have happened that would have violated that? Would you have allowed anything to happen that either of you would afterwards have to be ashamed about in real terms? I think the answer is obvious, you wouldn't have. You were more inclined to err on the side of caution. You did this even if this meant closing the door to being totally truthful with yourself. Isn't this what you did? You avoided the dimensions that you couldn't fully understand. Am I correct?"

I squeezed her hand in reply. "You know me better than I know myself," I replied moments later. "You are amazing!"

32

"There is no magic involved, Peter. I just see us from a higher level standpoint, as human beings. That's all I do. That's all I can do. And what results from that often amazes me too."

I shook my head again. "You are right. Nothing would have happened between Erica and I, that either of us would have had to be ashamed about. This wouldn't have been possible. I was too grateful for having met her, for having had the conversations with her that we had, and for the beautiful kind of person that she is. How could I have possibly hurt her or done anything degrading? I was so grateful just to be with her."

"Can you say then that you were grateful that she exists?" Helen asked.

"I still am, Helen. This grateful feeling has never gone away, or ever will," I replied. "She is still in my heart. Indeed, I am grateful that she exists, wherever she may be, even if I will never see her again. She has found a place in my thoughts. I am grateful for that. Do I make any sense?"

Helen didn't answer no, or yes. She said something to the effect that gratitude enables sovereignty to be. "But did you tell her that? There is so little gratitude for one-another's existence. We take each other for granted, and in the process we loose sight of our humanity. Without gratitude our lives become barren. People talk about Love, but they cannot conceal the ingratitude that causes those barren lives. I think your friend understands this, though she doesn't want to admit it. That is also why she doesn't see the flower garden correctly. I remember a verse of an old hymn, Peter, which I have remembered for a long time. It goes like this:

"A grateful heart a garden is, where there is always room, for every lovely Godlike grace, to come to perfect bloom."

"That's beautiful," I said. I was tempted to kiss her spontaneously for it. I was going to say that this verse is as beautiful as she is, and more so because she said those words.

33

"People talk about respecting one-another," Helen cut off my dreaming. "Can you imagine how much brighter the world would be, if people would be honestly grateful for one-another's existence? I think most people are grateful for one-another, although they rarely realize that. When I confront them with it, they are shocked, but a while later they agree. And when they do agree, their life becomes brighter."

Our world soon became brighter in a different way, in a less important way, as we reached the brightly-lit Railway Station Plaza. She pointed to a tall building at the opposite end, which barely stood out against the black sky. The building looked like a modern hotel. A few windows were lit up.

As we came closer it became gradually apparent that this was a high-rise apartment, not a hotel. A hotel would have been logical right next to the Railway Station Plaza. As we came to it, the building appeared to be new. It had a brightly-lit entrance. It reflected the same air of elegance that she did.

She pointed out proudly that she lives on the top floor.

Chapter 4 - Living on the Top Floor

Her place wasn't as large as I had expected, but more beautiful than I had dared to imagine. An oak table stood in a dining nook, right beside a large window. Four elegant chairs surrounded the table.

The main room was largely taken up by a grand piano, an older model. The window in the main room extended nearly across the entire wall. It offered a sweeping view of the railway plaza below, a sea of glittering lights, backed by a dark park-like area in the distance.

On the wall next to the piano was a bookshelf located with birthday cards set up among glass ornaments. She told me that I should make myself feel at home, while she put the coffee on.

My attention was drawn to the birthday cards. One of them was apparently custom made. The creating artist had wished her a happy "forever-day" celebration, as he had called her birthday. Inside the card he had written, "To my precious Love, and my beautiful lover."

The care with which the apartment was arranged, testified to that great Love that the artist spoke of in the card, which was evident everywhere. It evidently extended also to her friends.

Since she hadn't returned from the kitchen, I ventured to join her there. The kitchen was located off to the side of the dining nook, where the oak table stood. She had left the sliding door to the kitchen partially open.

Almost in the last moment, just as I was about to enter, I noticed that she was crying. A letter lay in front of her on the table together with a small booklet that appeared to be a bankbook of some sort. She didn't notice me. Her head was bent low. Her hands partially covered her face. A crumpled paper napkin lay on the table. I turned back and looked out of the window again, waiting for her to deal with what was troubling her, giving her time.

Money troubles? I pondered. What else would she be in the bar for so late at night? Maybe somebody owed her and didn't pay her back. Maybe she had been waiting for this person in the pub, who stood her up, for which she was now in a state of crisis. Or maybe someone close whom she had trusted, had betrayed her. It usually hurts twice as bad, when trust is betrayed. Or, maybe she just lost her job and didn't know how to make ends meet. Or maybe she was just plain broke, or got robbed. I could think of a thousand reasons why people might cry over money. I had been there myself. I felt almost ashamed for how well I was being paid now in the diplomatic service, compared to most people who struggle every day to make ends meet. I had to laugh at myself as I remembered a time long ago, when I had been so broke that all I could afford to eat was a stick of cheese and some dry buns, that both had to be rationed out for a week, till the next payday came around. I had been too proud then to ask for help. It seemed easier to go hungry for a week.

I was startled out of my dreaming when I felt her touch on my shoulder. I turned around. I almost stared at her in surprise. She was a totally different person than the one I had seen just minutes earlier in the kitchen. She stood beside me, her head held high, no trace of tears, and her long hair neatly combed. She smiled and offered me some home made cookies on a plate.

"So you have come to learn what Love is," she said, still smiling.

She didn't talk about money, or made any requests for money, or even hinted that she was in trouble, as it appeared that she was.

I talked with her about Erica some more. I repeated that Erica was studying Love as a scientific discipline, like someone would study physics, but who could still not move with its demands from a certain point on. We didn't talk about the flower garden anymore.

"You were lucky that your friend was able to move as far as she did," said Helen. "Most people crawl into themselves much earlier, and close the door. Obedience has been the curse of humanity for more than a thousand years. That's when the real dark ages began. People were obedient slaves, lesser beings, humble and stupid, but this suddenly changed in the middle of the 1300s. That's when people began to discover themselves with a new vision, and with it, discover their true riches."

Helen suggested that we sit down in the "good room" to talk about this. She placed the cookies on a small side table next to the sofa where she asked me to sit. "Would you like a glass of port?" she asked. She didn't wait for an answer. She went to a nearby wall-mounted miniature buffet and brought two glasses out.

Helen stood tall on high-heeled shoes. Her long dark hair covered the top of her dress even though the top of the dress ended way below her shoulders. Her dress was black. She wore black sheer stockings. The stockings were not seamless by design. An artificial seam extended from her shoes all the way up as far as one could see, carefully set into a perfectly straight line.

She put the glasses down and smiled. As if nothing had happened, she looked away from me. She looked away quietly and smiled. No torrent of words flowed from her lips in protesting my incursion into the privacy of her world. She went back into the kitchen. Before she did, she turned around momentarily at the door, still smiling.

"Do you like Portuguese port?" she called back from the kitchen, as if this was an important question.

She brought out a large bottle of Portuguese port. The bottle was still sealed. She showed it to me. I simply nodded and smiled. The port wasn't important to me; she was the gem that paled everything.

"I think this particular brand will do great for a special occasion like this," she said, and took the bottle back. "I brought it back with me from a cultural exchange event. We can learn from the Portuguese; they know how to celebrate. I think we give ourselves far too few occasions when we feel it is appropriate to celebrate," she said. She opened the bottle with a high tech corkscrew, and filled the glasses herself. As she did this, she crouched down beside me, but carefully avoided eye contact, as if the resulting eye connection would pose a danger to the mental portal that was beginning to open with the unfolding intimacy of her closeness. However, her smile remained.

"It's a nice color, this one," she commented when she was finished filling the glasses. She handed one of the glasses to me.

The color of the port was as dark as port is, almost as dark as her stockings were that appeared even more prominent in the crouched position in which she tasted the port.

"It will do," she said. Then forced the cork back into the opened bottle. She handed the bottle to me. There was eye contact this time, brief as it was. It was a contact with her Soul so it seemed. It was a glimpse of a world that existed beyond the portal. It strengthened the view; it widened it.

The whole process of this voiceless communication became rather richly erotic, like an exciting ceremony of a distant culture that one barely understands, but that one can identify with as though one had been born into it. At least that's how the unfolding atmosphere appeared more and more in the way it touched a chord deep inside me that had been kept hidden so deep in the background that it appeared almost foreign now as its presence was felt again. What unfolded felt like a type of celebration that was gradually and slowly 'erupting' into life. But what were we celebrating? Were we celebrating just being alive?

Something was happening that I had long secretly challenged, that I couldn't deny its unfolding, or wanted to deny. I relished its promise. I was falling in Love again with still another woman. Wow! Two times on the same day! Wow!

I mentally slapped my face as if I needed to wake up. "Peter, don't do that!" said a voice from within. But the voice was overruled.

"What you are about to do, Peter, cheapens the closeness that you have felt towards Erica just a few hours ago, that you have treasured and still do, and probably will treasure forever," said the voice within. The voice seemed strong, but its argument hollow.

"Will the promising new eruption of Love cheapen anything?" I argued back at myself. "How can one aspect of Love, unfolding on top of another, cheapen and dilute anything? Should it not rather enrich both aspects, and this in a manner that the end result is greater than the sum of both parts?"

I began to smile to myself that I had won this argument. But had I really won?

I wondered what Erica might have said, being the level-headed scientist that she was, or what the professor might have said in the pub. I reasoned that the professor would likely have ordered a glass of soda water with ice and poured an ounce of Whisky into it. That would have been his style. "Now taste that!" I heard him say to me in my mind. And I would have tasted it. Then he would have poured another ounce of Whisky into it. "Now taste it again!" I heard him say. "Has the addition diluted the first taste? Or has the taste become more powerful?"

"And what would Erica, the scientist, have said?" I questioned myself.

Ah, that one was easy to answer. "How can Love be a poison to itself?" I heard her ask me in return. "How can the restricting of Love help us with learning to be more loving, to love more fully, as we all should?" That's what Erica might have said. She might have added, "Does increasing our austerity make the gold more precious that we have, or does increasing our austerity merely enhance the resulting poverty?" I heard her say to me in my mind, that we should be in Love more fully in order that we would love ourselves more fully. "Don't we have ample reasons to do this for the wondrous humanity that we have and all its rich dimensions that we share?"

I heard her say to me, "Peter, embrace Love at every chance that life presents, by which loving becomes more diffusive, and by which the darkness of our days goes away."

I heard Erica in my mind, add as if it were a comment to my expanding loving, "I envy you, Peter."

Chapter 5 – What do You Wish for Most in Your Life?

"What do you wish for the most in your life?" Helen broke the silence that I drifted into.

I was startled. I hesitated. "I really don't know what I wish for the most?" I said finally. "Do I wish for a house, or a better one? No! I don't wish for that. I have a house that is perfectly adequate. Do I wish for an interesting job that provides sufficient income? No! I have that too. Do I wish for a loving wife? I have that already. Do I wish for romance? I had that also. I had a beautifully romantic day."

I shook my head. "Isn't this silly? You asked me a simple question, what do you want most in life, and I can't answer. I could say that I wished for sex, but if I did, I could have had plenty of that for a twenty-dollar bill or whatever the going price is. So, I really don't know what the answer is to your question."

"There was something that you deeply wanted in the pub and couldn't find there, something that brought you to the pub in the first place," she said. "I don't think you came there in the middle of the night to learn about politics, or to be scared by it even more that you had been before."

I nodded. "Sure, something had been missing, Helen. That wonderfully bright day that I had shared with Erica had ended with a sad failure," I said after a moment of hesitation. "Something didn't happen, that perhaps should have happened. We had the most wonderful day together as two human beings embracing each other in Love, but it ended with us facing a barrier. It ended with a line drawn in the sand. In a way I was clad at the time that the line was laid down. It closed the door to a difficult territory that seemed both beautiful, but also immensely challenging. It seemed easier to avoid the challenge than to deal with it. Isn't that what the whole world is doing? I think the challenge was far greater than anything that either of us was prepared to deal with, so that running away from it was the sanest response for the occasion."

Helen just laughed. "You are right on this one. The whole world is using this excuse. That's the oldest excuse in the book. That's why nothing gets resolved. That is why we have built tens of thousands of nuclear bombs to blow ourselves up with. You are saying then that you are wishing for something that the whole world is wishing for, that the problems would simply go away, or that somebody else would solve them for you. How noble of you!" said Helen and began to grin.

"I can't deny that sex was an element. It always is an element of what I would wish to be involved in," I replied, "though in the case with Erica it probably wouldn't have been a big thing in comparison with what we already had. Still I had been hoping till the last moment that our joining hands would include a sexual touch and that beyond it something greater than mere sex would emerge. I was hoping for a kind of intimacy that makes our sexual embracing something special that only human beings have the capacity to develop, something in which we are uniquely human. It would then have the potential to be something like a miracle that unfolds when our thinking is raised to a higher level where such 'miracles' actually become real. The whole human dimension is like a miracle in that way, isn't it? Maybe that is what I should be wishing for. What really defines us as human beings takes us beyond what we can find in any other form of life, in the known Universe. As human beings we are defined by a great profusion of 'miracles,' unfolding as art, science, music, literature, beauty, creativity, compassion, loving, generosity, honesty, to mention just a few. I suspect that sex also has this kind of a higher dimension, if only we could find it. I think we should look at sex as a unique human dimension that lies far above the level of the animal dimension of it as a means for procreation. Unfortunately, the lower form of sex, is what society is commonly focusing on. I suspect, that this is what Erica had felt impelled to close the door to. Maybe she had to do this because the higher dimension hadn't been built where sex becomes meaningful in a constructive way. I also suspect that we will never experience that higher dimension, for as long as we find it easier to close the door to it, than to take up the challenge to explore this higher level dimension and its advanced principles. The professor suggested that sex has a profound purpose in the higher human dimension, to bring us into the realm of the Principle of the General Welfare. I think I was in the pub to ponder where the boundary lies between the possible and the miraculous," I added. "I suppose; I was dreaming a dream that might always remain but a dream."

"Aren't we human beings a peculiar lot?" said Helen. "You were hoping for something that the whole of humanity is hoping for, a kind of universal closeness. The reality is that you were hoping for something that is easily fulfilled. Still, we find it terribly hard to help one-another to take those simple steps across the barriers that we have built up over centuries against the fulfillment of our needs. I find this so often, Peter," she added quietly. She almost sighed.

"Perhaps it is fear," I said to her. "We've become locked into a prison of fear, like Hamlet in Shakespeare's tragedy, who couldn't take that one simple step that he most desired, and had the authority to take. Perhaps it is fear of the unknown country, for which we have stayed away from it for centuries, because public opinion says, don't cross that line. We even teach this to our children. We tell them; don't cross that line; don't go into the forest; be aware of the wolf; be careful Little Red Riding-Hood."

Helen was sitting next to me on the sofa when we spoke about Hamlet and Little Red Riding-Hood. After a while we said nothing more to each other. Evidently she allowed me time to sort myself out. She may have realized that those movements in thought that the unfolding of this new situation inspired, could have far reaching consequences for good, if they were allowed to unfold and thereby provide a basis that we could build on. Indeed, we could build on the riches of that wider world that Erica has already opened up and that Helen now provided an even larger horizon for, that beckoned me to move forward. What could come from that building might even prevent my regression back into the old and narrow world of thinking, or even a deeper regression into its poverty, with harsher limits than those that I had been struggling to break away from.

Helen explained after a long period of silence, that after the great financial crash in 1345, and the Black Death plague had had ravished Europe two years later and killed a third of its population, some people

43

began to focus more and more on the value of the human being. This value was discerned more and more against the emptiness of chaos. It was found as something precious, reflecting a wondrous light that pervades the nature of our humanity, which became recognized as the real nature of mankind. Especially some of the younger people could recognize this light within. Helen told me that some young boys who had been taught in the monasteries to read and write, in order to help the monks to copy ancient manuscripts, had thereby become familiar with the humanist discoveries of Plato and with Plato's scientific method of discovery. Thereby they grew up to become accomplished independent thinkers of their own. Out of this background the first 'teaching' institution emerged, the famous teaching order called the Brotherhood of the Common Life. It encouraged students to replicate in their own mind the discoveries of the pioneers of humanity. It focused on the process of learning the process of discovery itself.

"With this process a new perception of the human being emerged," Helen continued. "The learning of the art of making discoveries even revolutionized religion. The Platonic thinking process challenged the old notion that the Holy Spirit flows from God to humanity, via the Son, as an intermediary. People began to see this hierarchical model as a model that justified imperial rule. In the unfolding Golden Renaissance, a new perception came to light that had its root in the original Christian perception, where humanity was seen as being directly the reflected image of God and thereby of great worth, with the Christ not being an intermediary, but being the Exemplar of it. This perception attributed enormous value to each individual human being. It changed the world. It was this elevated perception that became synonymous with the Renaissance. It created the foundation for a deep-seated self-loving in humanity. People became more aware of their capability as thinkers and creators. They also became more respectful of each other, and thereby became closer to each other, and more cooperative with each other. Out of this revolutionary development the Principle of the General Welfare was born, and with it the concept of the nation-state, in which this principle would be expressed. The imperial-state didn't allow such an expression. A new type of state was required, in which Love was no longer recognized as a hierarchical flow from a superior being to a lesser being, but was recognized as a lateral flow between equals that combined God and mankind as one, and mankind with each other. With this new view unfolded the people's self-loving, their loving of the truth of the humanity that they all shared and were a part of. By this kind of development in looking at the truth, Love became a totally different thing. People became connected laterally, as we do right here. But Peter, if Love unfolds laterally, it has to be universal. Thus, ultimately, Love exists only in the form of universal Love. Any other form of it is a distortion of it. Can you understand this?"

I reached for the port. I looked at her face, into her eyes, drank in her smile. Yes, I understood some of it. "I love your definition of Love as a lateral flow." I said with a smile.

"You love it because it is true," she added. "That's what I think."

"I can sense that it is true," I said and smiled back. "This means I now have a solid basis for loving you. There is something wonderful about you that I appreciate deep in my heart, and it isn't all sexual."

"But some of it is sexual," she replied. "Be honest!"

"Oh, a lot of it is. What you are as a woman, and a beautiful woman at that, seems to be a part of my humanity too, otherwise I wouldn't have this warm cuddly feeling just looking at you. What motivates this response is already located in me. In responding to it, I can't help feeling amazed. I am amazed at the great Intelligence that organized the Universe, and this fantastic phenomenon of Life that now includes human living. It's phenomenal, isn't it, considering how perfect it all is in its wondrous complexity. The Intelligence that is reflected in our being gave us two legs to walk with, two eyes to see with, and two sexes to develop intimacies with each other. Each aspect seems to have an equally amazing purpose. Obviously the Intelligence of the Universe didn't give us sex merely for procreation. Sure sex is an ideal means for genetically enhancing the diversity of our species. But I think there is far more to it. There is something about it that affects also the social and universal realm. The professor pointed out that in cultures were sex has been mutilated, whereby its higher functions were diminished, the development of civilization stopped and was reversed. It appears to me therefore that the great Intelligence that is reflected in this wonder of human living, that we are a part of, has given us the dimension of sex as a kind of foundation for developing a sense of closeness with one-another that more and more reflects the lateral model that you spoke of, which has started to come into light with the Renaissance. It appears to me even that this developing sense of social and national intimacies, and their unfolding economic potential for civilization to prosper, might be the greater purpose for the sexual intimacies that are built into the human system. These private intimacies are expanding into all sorts of larger intimacies, like family intimacies, neighborhood intimacies, cooperative economic intimacies, and even national and political intimacies. We see this expanding pattern reflected in people's sense of a nation and a world of cooperating sovereign nation-states. So I don't think we are dealing with anything trivial when the subject of sex comes to the forefront. As for me, I find its demands as powerful imperatives, otherwise I wouldn't be here and be looking at you with a smile and feel al cuddly inside, and this so much so that I don't want to take my eyes off you."

I paused and began to laugh suddenly.

She waved a finger at me, apparently in jest, and began to laugh likewise.

"It's true, what I said, and I couldn't keep my eyes off Erica either, as I come to think of it," I said to her. "But this really isn't a laughing matter, is it? I feel so cuddly just looking at you. That's built into the human system. Some purpose impels this. But what is it? I think something greater than us is involved here that impels this. Maybe the purpose behind this is far greater than we can imagine. It seems to me that life is a great unexplored country that promises as yet unseen blessing with sex being a part of it."

Helen just smiled.

"What I said is all evident as far as I can tell, because nothing else makes sense," I said.

46

"If sex existed exclusively for procreation, a lot of nations would have died out by now, especially those whose culture demands the physical removal of their people's sexual sensitivity in both men and women," said Helen. "The victims of those cultures have nothing left of their genitalia that generates the supposedly necessary sexual drive for procreation. Nevertheless, those nations still exist, the procreation continues in spite of the mutilations, and this has continued down this road for thousands of years. Only civilization has been collapsing in this background."

"This perplexed the professor too," I said to her.

"The simple fact that this perplexing thing happens," said Helen, "tells us that the human sexual sensitivity has a much greater purpose than procreation, a purpose that has not yet been recognized. What this purpose is, may be found in the factor that sets the victimized nations apart from normal nations. In my estimation this factor is not surprising. Nor is it hidden. In fact, it is universally apparent. All the victimized nations have one thing in common. They have functionally become nations of slaves. Economically they are radically underdeveloped. Socially they are torn by strive, violence, and often civil war. And politically they are easily manipulated as if they had no sense of being a part of a nation. They are prone to bow to whoever would be king over them. So, Helen, if that is the evidence that we see associated with a nation or culture that has excised the sexual sensitivity out of its people, by which that human intimacy is prevented from becoming a factor, I am wondering what powerful factor the sexual sensitivity and resulting intimacy really serve in the natural system of our humanity."

"If sexual sensitivity isn't required for procreation, and procreation continues without it," I interjected, "then we need to look for what we loose when the sexual sensitivity is removed. The professor says that the lack of it causes a decrepit society in the most crucial respects. Since he is apparently right, the factor of sexual sensitivity, developing intimacy, comes to light as an immensely vital one for the very existence of civilization. This factor might ultimately prove to be more crucial than procreation itself, for mankind's existence as a whole. In this case all the world's problems, as far as I can tell, from nuclear war to economic chaos, appear to be all forms of derivatives of society's insanity in trashing this vital factor."

Helen leaned over and kissed me. "Congratulations!" she said to me holding her hand out.

I returned the gesture.

"Do you realize that you have recognized and articulated in ten minutes what I have tried for years to get the professor to understand?" said Helen. "I have pushed this subject so extensively that it has become the talk of the university. Most people there don't know me, but they do know the professor who now speaks of these things. Unfortunately, with his reputation, the people at the university think he is nuts, when he speaks about the circumcision as a danger to civilization."

"I think he is too bitter to understand the connection this has with Love, that is reflected therein," I replied. "Maybe he is a victim of the circumcision himself."

"I don't think so," said Helen. "However, I think he is too scared of what he already knows of the consequences that he sees unfolding, to trust Love as a sufficient element of Principle to get us out of that mess. He is scared of the Truth that he sees fading from sight, because with it comes the responsibility of facing up to it, truthfully, and reversing the trend. That, Peter, can be terribly scary. And in that respect he is a coward. His cowardice is eating him on the inside. It is gnawing on the soul."

"I think that what he said to me is true," I answered quietly. "This, all by itself, means that he has every right to be scared. We all should be scared about what today's society is doing to itself."

Helen shook her head. "This kind of thinking is a trap," she said. "It implies that we don't have the capacity to change the world. The Renaissance once overturned this kind of thinking. Just look at us, we are an example that the world can change. We were both despondent less than one hour ago, sitting in that pub, both for our own reason. Now, look at us. We are both smiling. You feel cuddly inside. You even say you are in Love. I have a warm feeling for you too. Hasn't our world changed?"

"You are a genius," I said and leaned over and kissed her back. "You are totally right. One idea can change the world. Maybe sex has a lot more to do with that than we dare to acknowledge. Maybe we are all cowards in this sense. But we are waking up and are becoming a bit more daring, you and I. It appears to be natural that an honest responding to sex inspires a lot of loving. Shouldn't we recognize sex then as also being a profound aspect of Love?"

Helen didn't answer. She got up and brought the letter from the kitchen that I had seen earlier. "This is another proof that a single idea can change a person's life."

Chapter 6 – Economics of a Love Letter

"Is this the reason you were in the pub?" I asked. "I saw you cry over that letter," I said, and put my arm around her.

She bent her head down again. "Yes," she said quietly. "The letter says that a day ago a close friend of mine had three fingers chopped off his right hand."

"That's barbaric," I muttered. "What kind of a country is this where such a thing can happen?"

She began to laugh. "You are thinking of Islamic justice. This doesn't happen here. My friend was injured in an industrial accident in a book binding shop. He was brushing some cuttings away at the edge trimmer to get rid of some trimmings that the vacuum system hadn't picked up. The interlocks must have been disabled. We don't know what had tripped the switch."

"No wonder you were shook up," I said quietly. "What will happen to him now?"

Helen explained that he was extremely lucky. "He lost mostly the fingertips. The cuts were clean and were repairable. Nothing had to be amputated." She said that he would be well cared for by the state and wouldn't loose his job either, as this might have happened in the West. She said, she couldn't help crying though, because the man was also a concert pianist by profession. "Music is his life, Peter." She said that he would probably never be able to play the piano again as a concert pianist. "Nevertheless something happened tonight in my thinking about the tragedy," she added. "The idea came that my friend would likely be able to play the violin in concert. He had talked about playing the violin some day, except he had never been able to get enough money together to buy a good-enough instrument for concert work. I don't have enough money myself to buy him one, but I have a little that I can spare. It won't amount to anything more than just a gesture. Still, that gesture will mean a great deal to him in this critical time. I cried, because I realized that I am able to do this for him, which might change his life. Can you see now how one idea can radically change a person's life, and all life on the planet if it unfolds evermore fully?"

"We can change the world that way," I added some moments later. "You are right; the professor's dire predictions don't have to come true. If we can solve this little problem with an advanced idea, why can't we solve the great problems of the world by applying the principle of the idea further? Maybe we can solve the deep problems that disable entire nations."

Helen didn't answer. She took the letter back to the kitchen. I heard her filling the kettle. When she returned I handed her three thousand East German Marks in cash, all in five hundred Mark notes. "This should help a bit," I added.

"No, I can't accept that," she said and handed the money back.

I didn't take it back. I told her that I really didn't need it. I explained that all foreign agents were required by the state to exchange a fixed amount of money each day. The amount that is required is roughly the equivalent to what one would spend on a five-star hotel in New York, meals included. I assured her that I wouldn't mind living in a low cost motel by the highway for the duration of my stay, if doing so would put the money to use where it can really make a difference for someone in a crisis, like that of her friend. I also told her that a rule had come to mind that I had loved as a child. I had almost forgotten it. It is based on the fact that we all live in this world together. We can do beautiful things and make our world beautiful, or we can do terrible things and make our world intolerable. "I was delighted as a child when I was able to say to myself before going to bed at night, that I had made a difference in making the world a lovelier place to be in. That's lateral loving, isn't it?" I added.

I explained that I didn't really need to stay in a five-star hotel. I urged her to keep the money for her friend. "I would rather stay in a cheap place and eat with ordinary people in an ordinary restaurant," I said to her, "and live like ordinary people do, and take the money that I won't have to spend that way, to help someone in need with it. That's the kind of stuff I had always been proud of when I was a kid. It seems I've been brought up that way. It's time to get back to being proud for embracing what is good. It's not a sacrifice then for me to do this. It's a nice thing to do that I will probably always cherish when I think of it in future years. Isn't that how we brighten the world?"

Helen looked at the money, then looked at me, and began to cry again. "Thank you," she said. She said it with new tears in her eyes. "Thank you from the bottom of my heart." She took the money and placed it in an envelope together with a note that said something about a violin. She added a check of her own and sealed the envelope. She wrote the man's name on it and signed it, and asked me to sign it as well.

I signed it gladly. I signed my full name, Peter A. VanDerMere. I encircled my first name.

"Maybe if it wasn't for the closeness that comes with people's intimacy that flows from sex, your response and mine might have been quite different," she said.

"It might not have opened the door to the next stage of responding, such as his response that will now give him his life back," I said to her. "Isn't it amazing how powerfully effective and uplifting an honest response to sex can become?"

"I can agree with you on that," she said. "Sex is an expression of Love, a gift of the Universe, and a vital one for civilization." She began to laugh with the tears still flowing.

We embraced each other for a long time after saying this. Something wonderful had happened to our world that inspired this embrace. Our embrace lasted until our tears stopped and the water kettle was whistling in the kitchen.

Helen returned to the kitchen. "And here, I thought I would be teaching you about Love," she called back to me from the kitchen. "Instead you taught me."

"But you have started it all with your history lesson, and by being your wonderful self," I said to her as, I followed her into the kitchen to be closer to her. "I hope you don't mind me invading your kitchen," I said, as I entered. "I am still in awe of what you have said. I am in Love with the wonderful person that you are. I amazed at the good that you have already brought out in me. If anyone had predicted this back at the pub, I would have laughed. What is happening here is revolutionary," I added. "It is as revolutionary, as you are beautiful. I am in Love with you for something that seems to be greater than all of us, which is wonderfully reflected in you." I ventured for another kiss.

She didn't answer me. She merely smiled. She got the tea started and began to prepare us some sandwiches for a late-night snack. She put jars of olives on the counter, three types, and butter, several types of sausage, and rye bread.

"Loving means more," she said while making the sandwiches, unwrapping the butter. "Loving begins with loving oneself as a human being," she said. "Your friend Erica hadn't discovered that yet, because she didn't know a thing abut the deep connection between sex and Love. Our loving begins when we discover in ourselves the wonders of our humanity. Then we discover beauty in our Soul. We discover joy, art, wisdom, and scientific awareness. Human loving begins when we discover ourselves as being creators in a 'divine' Universe, and the brightest stars of life that has developed out of Life's long history on this planet. We begin to be in Love with ourselves, when we see in us the image of God. When this happens we cannot help, but to be in Love with one-another, and to be truly loving. People speak of loving, but this is often a front as they have something else in mind. They say to a person, I love you, but they really should say, I am compelled to be near you because I want you to brighten my life; I want you to give me what I have not found in myself;

I want you to fill my emptiness. This isn't Love, Peter. This is a game of exploitation. This is crude selfishness that has nothing to do with Love.

"But you are not like that, Peter," she continued. "Still, you say you love me. You say it with your eyes. You say with your eyes that you want to touch me, and that you want to touch me as a woman, intimately. And so you should. When we begin to be in Love, Peter, we find ourselves to be compelled to uplift the world around us. We are compelled to uplift one-another to a higher level of joy, to a higher appreciation for who and what we are, and to a greater honesty and openness, where we enrich one-another out of the depth of our humanity that we all share. When we begin to do this, then loving is no longer a game, but something that flows heart to heart, something that threads through history, something that has shaped history and even darkened it when it was prevented. Without understanding Love, one cannot understand history. You have already hinted at this. In Love there is joy, and sex is a factor. And the three together are one, with sex being a vital factor by which we enrich one-another in Love. Of course we embrace one-another then, even as we embrace ourselves. Do you agree that this is what loving is?"

I didn't know how to answer. I agreed! But I had never lived in that dimension. To say, yes, would have been dishonest. It would not have been born out of my own experiences. I answered with a nod instead. I said that I was just beginning to fall in Love again. I proved it with a kiss. I said, "Thank you for helping me." I think Helen recognized the honesty involved.

Helen continued making the sandwiches, while we talked. "Something to go with the tea," she said, when she noticed my being surprised by the careful preparation.

The tea was peppermint tea. The sandwiches were made of dark rye-bread served with sweet pickles and three kinds of olives on the side, all beautifully arranged. She arranged them with the same care that was reflected in everything about her, including in the way she dressed; the way she kept her hair; and the way she made me feel comfortable.

"You said that sex is a vital factor in history," I said to her to get the conversation redirected back to it.

"Don't you agree with what I said about history?" she said, after she had sliced the last pickle. She turned around and leaned against the counter.

"Did you know that Hitler is reported to have said in private circles that a fascist state must never teach real history, because when real history is being taught, a fascist state would have a revolution on its hand? I think this statement shows Hitler's real color as a wise, but also a despicable person, the worst kind that one can imagine. But he was not alone in that. He feared a society understanding history, because real history gives people a vision of the great achievements of mankind and also of the consequences of its failures. Every empire fears this awareness in society. The masters of empire know that a society understanding universal history furnishes an open door for it to discover the native freedom of the human being and the tragedy that flows from denying it. But where does one begin the exploration of that freedom? In order to understand the universal history of mankind, one needs to start at the beginning of civilization. This, Peter, takes us far back in time all the way to the dynasties of the Pharaohs in Egypt where the freedom of mankind was brutally denied. Ancient Egypt might have been the first of the large-scale slavery empires. Slaves are human beings of course, and human beings will naturally react when their humanity is massively violated. It appears therefore that this natural reaction became a problem for the Pharaohs that they responded to overcome. The problem was that a self-alert society doesn't lend itself easily to slavery. The Pharaohs were likely 'intensely' scared of the slaves, but they also needed the slaves. So, Peter, how do you think they solved their problem?"

"I think I know where this is leading," I said. "But I can't be sure. This has something to do with sex, since you are responding to my question that is focused on sex. Also the professor had a sense of such a connection existing."

Helen nodded and smiled. "Actually, we can only guess at the details," said Helen. "But we do have historic pictographs inscribed in stone going as far back as 2,500 BC, that suggest that the Egyptian masters had performed the circumcision on their male slaves. The masters of the slaves had cut away the male slaves sexual sensitivity and thereby prevented the natural intimacy from maturing that they would otherwise have had with their women. The Egyptian masters thereby prevented the consequent closeness of the slaves with one another, both individually and as a community. Diminishing the slaves' sexual sensitivity thereby gave the slaves more time to do their assigned work. But as you might guess, improving the work-efficiency of the slaves wasn't the dynasty's real interest in this case. They had a different purpose in mind. They had a different target. The real target that the masters of Egypt had evidently been aiming at was the Principle of the General Welfare that flows from the natural social intimacy that is rooted in sexual intimacy. The rulers evidently knew, perhaps from bitter experience, that whenever this principle is allowed to develop in a society, the process of slavery ends. The Pharaohs couldn't allow this. They addressed the problem in the only manner that it could have been addressed, by intervening at the root. That, apparently is how the circumcision began 4,500 years ago. Of course what the Pharaoh's had recognized then is still being recognized today by the modern masters of empire. The Principle of the General Welfare is still being regarded as the greatest poison to any process of slavery anywhere. Consequently, the circumcision is still being performed, and for the original reason."

"This was probably also the reason why they mutilated the slave's women as well," I interjected. "According to the professor, that's what the Pharaohs had done. Improving the slave-women's work efficiency obviously hadn't been a big factor in early Egypt, but inhibiting the sexual intimacy that opens the gates to the Principle of the General Welfare, was evidently a big factor. I think they waged a war against this principle in order to shut it down, thereby shutting down a dangerous factor that any empire fears. Evidently that had been a big factor for the Pharaohs. For what other reason would the Pharaohs have infibulated their slave women? From an economic standpoint, it makes no sense to do that. The procedure is too brutal, and the outcome too debilitating, and probably often deadly as well."

"Oh yes, the infibulation of women stands among the most brutal crimes that were ever dreamed up against humanity. It may be the worst torture that one can imagine," said Helen quietly. "It tares one's heart just to think of it. Those were primitive times, and the methods were primitive. The operators ripped, cut, and scraped out the women's clitoris in which a woman's sexual sensitivity is located. But the Pharaohs didn't leave it with that, because the 'danger' for sexual intimacy might have still remained to some degree. Consequently, they cut away the women's entire external vulva. They evidently saw themselves impelled to do this, because as you know yourself, the very sight of a woman's vulva inspires intimate sexual feelings in men. The Pharaohs evidently felt that this 'danger' had to be stopped for the protection of their empire."

"I wonder if you know how right you are," I interjected. "Just go to any strip joint and look at the men's faces. Their smiles become brighter when the vulva appears on the scene. They literally come to see the vulva. They stare and smile. I have yet to meet a man who isn't moved with a fuzzy feeling in some fashion at the sight of a vulva."

"That is why the Pharaohs had to remove it as a 'threat,' by cutting and scraping every bit of the vulva away. They cut it all off and sowed what remained of the outer lips together with thorns. Evidently this brutal procedure effectively ended all intimacies, and any potential for the development of the Principle of the General Welfare among the slaves. Thus the slaves were conditioned to remain slaves, even to become 'better' slaves. The Pharaoh's empire proved to be safe after that. Obviously, a mutually isolated society never causes a revolt of the kind that the Pharaohs might have experienced at an earlier point. They probably responded to the logic of experience to prevent this from happening again. It appears, perhaps, that as a measure for breaking down even the remotest social connection, the masters of empire have forced the slave-women to perform the torturous infibulation on each other. At least this became a tradition that is still being practiced to the present day. For centuries the mutilation of women, that had been demanded by the imperial system, and had been mostly carried out by the women on each other, had assured the survival of the power of dynasties, which were all built to some degree on the slavery system."

"This horror story then is what the glory of ancient Egypt was built on!" I commended. "Evidently they didn't just capture people as ready-made slaves since natural slaves don't exist. They captured people and modified them to become slaves through and through."

Helen nodded. "As I said, the process still continues to the present day." Helen spoke quietly now as if the soften the impact thereby. "A hundred million women are victims of these kinds of sexual mutilation worldwide. Not all of the mutilations are as extreme as the infibulation, but the extreme procedure that the Pharaohs started, still continues. It remains the major part of the tragedy, and the Pharaohs as the source of it is still being acknowledged. The infibulation of women is still being referred to as the pharaonic procedure. And so, the brutality continues, because nothing has fundamentally changed. We still have that old political system remaining in the world that the Pharaohs have created. It is still here in spite of the liberation of mankind that started with the Golden Renaissance. We have two systems now. One is called the Nation-State system. Under this system people live free and fulfilling lives. This system is squarely built on the Principle of the General Welfare. That's what the Nation-State becomes the very expression of. The other system is the old system of empire. It's the slavery system. The Nation-State system is under attack today all around the world, by the masters of empire. Consequently, the slave-creating process still continues, Peter. Few nations exist today as sovereign Nation-States. The masters of empire are still fighting against the same principle that the Pharaohs fought against, and the are just as scared today of it today, as the Pharaohs were then. The masters of empire are determined to prevent the Principle of the General Welfare from coming to life. They are fighting to squash it at all cost, just as the Pharaoh's had done. Only a few minor aspects have changed, between then and now. The infibulation has given way to the far more powerful modern forms of sexual isolation. The modern forms are specifically designed to prevent a new sense of social intimacy from unfolding, which would create a new renaissance through the eruption of the Principle of the General Welfare. But as I understand the principle involved, the empire's war against this principle is all for naught. The platform that empire is built on is becoming increasingly self-defeating. Empire is a political system that reaches out to steal from its neighbors. It does this in ever-widening circles now. It is obvious that when it has depleted what it is feeding on, it dies. It is important to understand this, because this part of history is common to all forms of empire, and the trend isn't over yet. In fact, the insanity that makes the system of empire self-defeating, is intensifying."

"Oh, but empire still rules," I interjected. "I wish it wasn't. But instead of diminishing, it is getting bigger."

"History warns us that when nothing remains for the empire to loot, the empire dies, but before it dies, it becomes increasingly fascist and takes society down with it," said Helen. "The death of empire is near, Peter. It cannot be avoided. But society is in greater danger than ever, because of its being linked into it. Society is in danger, because it is still a society of slaves. It has lost its self-interest and remains slavishly locked to the system of empire. Modern western society defends the system of empire even at the cost of loosing its civilization. That's the mark of a slave society, Peter. Sure, the infibulation is fading, but the circumcision is on the rise, especially in America. Seventy percent of the US mail population has already been victimized by it and turned into better slaves. Most of that happened in the postwar period. The effect this had is astounding. Just open your eyes, Peter, and look at how America has changed during the postwar period. The circumcision has turned America from being the giant that it was at the end of the war, into a slave to the empire, that it sells its heart and soul to support. America has become doomed thereby. That's the effect when the foundation is being destroyed that sex provides as a starting platform for social intimacies, reflected in national and cultural intimacies. All of today's empires are now built on the circumcision, and they are insanely fighting each other and are threatening everyone on the planet in the course of it. Nevertheless, the system of empire is in the process of disintegrating. The consequences of the collapse are truly enormous, because the empire and its insanity have become enormous. My point is that the scope of the consequences that we now face, gives us a sense of how important the sexual intimacies truly are to civilization."

"What we see happening now makes the modern master of empire far worse than the Pharaohs had been," I interjected.

Helen nodded. "In the modern world, empire is a slime mould," said Helen. "It has spread itself across the globe under the heading of globalization and cultural freedom. This means it has given itself the freedom to mutilate almost the entire human landscape as far as its tentacles can reach. From what I see happening, the masters of empire and their slaves didn't just loot everything in sight, which is bad enough, but they also cut deep into the very heart of the human system and have destroyed its integrity. Now the whole world is in danger, because of that."

"We are now facing World War III coming out of the Middle East," I said quietly. "The clash is not about religion. We have three mutilated societies brought together there, which are presently being setup against each other, facing each other with rage. That's the mark of insanity. That's the old British Empire strategy on a larger scale. I'm afraid my own country is the worst of that triad of insanity that grew out of the circumcision that is coming together there in the Middle East, which the British Empire wants to activate to blow the world apart. The war cries are already heard, shrill voices reflecting the sheer insanity of a disconnected people fighting each other in arenas, where nothing has any connection at all with human living. I am afraid that you may be right, that our people in America are being set up as slaves to be fighting other slaves in a Roman-style circus. What is now unfolding in the Middle East is not a battle between human beings. It is a battle between the slaves of circumcised cultures who had their humanity mutilated, and made ineffective. But I fail to see how we can win the world back and prevent this madness from progressing to its final stage that no one will likely survive. Without a profound sense of history, which the modern people in America lack, people have nothing to fall back on that would rescue them from their impending doom. As you pointed out, almost our entire nation has become slaves in the hands of empire. Don't we have any hope left? If we have, I don't see it. The professor saw no hope either."

"I would say you already know the answer, because as you said yourself, America's survival rests with its people's understanding the universal history of mankind," said Helen. She didn't smile this time. "The universal history of mankind is also the universal history of Love coming to light," she said moments later. "That's the key element that breaks the deadlock, Peter."

She paused to let me digest the idea.

Chapter 7 – When History was not Important

"In the early times of the Pharaohs, history was not important," Helen continued. "The people that were taken to become slaves had no great humanist achievements in their past that would inspire them to rebuild their natural tendency towards the Principle of the General Welfare. This development was just beginning to unfold. The early slaves probably didn't even know what a great treasure had been ripped away from them as a means for them becoming subjective slaves. The sexual mutilation was likely imposed shortly after birth, or at an early age. In this way most of them never knew what they lost. They never knew what the potential of a normal human being is, living in a normal society. Of course this argument doesn't hold water anymore in today's age, especially for America, that has had a proud history as the bastion of freedom and the beacon of liberty, as it was once known in many parts of the world."

"In this case I would say that the history of America should apply to mankind as a whole, as that of an exemplar of the freedoms that can be gleamed by stepping away from the sphere of empire," I interjected. "Mankind as a whole has gone through incredibly bright periods that were all built on the Principle of the General Welfare. America was founded on the intellectual shoulders of the great humanist giants that stood at the center of those bright periods. These were mostly located in Europe. In this sense the USA is essentially a leading edge European creation. America is the end result of two periods of renaissance happening in Europe. America's founding is these renaissance pioneers' gift to mankind, with the attached responsibility, to maintain this gift."

"That is why understanding universal history is an absolutely vital resource for mankind in today's troubled world, as a means for pulling itself out of its present trap, and for getting back on track," said Helen. "By looking at universal history, one invariably becomes a world-historic participant, Peter, rather than a bystander. One becomes inspired to recognize the trap that has disabled the world, and to break it open. That's Love coming to light. Sexual intimacy is evidently designed to play a part in it, perhaps even a major part. To be in Love means that one is a world-historic person fighting for the Principle of the General Welfare, by promoting all aspects that promote it. Nothing less will do, Peter. This means that we all need to explore history and let its logic guide our actions. In doing so we need to look at the great developments in the world towards ever greater freedoms, and the development of the real riches of mankind, and then note what had been done by the hired traitors to destroy those grand achievements for the sake of protecting empires. In this context, society will discover that America has been invaded by the circumcision, for the sake of empire. In that case, the invasion of America started at the end of World War II. The world of Islam has been invaded in the same manner some time earlier. The original Islam doesn't require the circumcision, and so forth. The poison has been injected into the Islamic world quietly over time, apparently by the masters of empire, whose tentacles reach far and wide, and cover much of the world. The males of the new American generations, and of the new Islamic generations, were given the exact same treatment that the slaves of the Pharaohs were subjected to. That is how America has lost its focus on the Principle of the General Welfare, the very principle that historically had been its hart and soul, without which the USA wouldn't even exist. And Islam too, has lost thereby some of its most precious elements. It might have lost all of what it had once been."

"Don't you think that it would be surprising if the masters of empire hadn't done this?" I Interjected. "I would be surprised if they hadn't done this especially to their arch enemy, America, that has been established as the world's foremost renaissance nation built on the Principle of the General Welfare. I think that is what we once were, at least by design. That's also what we lost. But it was taken away from us so gradually that nobody had any sense of the loss. Now, surprise, surprise, the Principle of the General Welfare is dead in America."

"The masters of empire must have studied the Pharaohs' methods well," said Helen. "Now that America has fallen, the evidence that I see is that the forces of empire have free reign almost across the whole world. Mankind's precious symbol for freedom, which the USA was, no longer exists, except by name. America is hated now for what it has come to represent."

"That is why I see no hope for the world now," I interjected. "With America having been betrayed to become a traitor against itself, and to become the world's foremost fighter against the Principle of the General Welfare, I am afraid that China, Russia, and India, even if they all banded together, wouldn't have the strength to turn back the rising tide of empire. Nor could they isolate themselves against it. They need America. They need it to become again, what it was once was. The key for rescuing mankind evidently lies in rescuing America from the trap of its slavery. But, Helen, I don't think this can be done with Love alone. If the circumcision, which as you say underlies the entire enslaving process, cannot be physically undone, what hope do we have? The circumcision is permanent. Once a person's sexual sensitivity is cut away, the intimacy no longer happens, and as the result over time, the sense of the people's intimacy as a nation does no longer exist. And that is where we are. The Principle of the General Welfare is now laughed at, even in America. The entire American culture has become enslaved to the empire's money, since America isn't sovereign even over its currency anymore."

Helen nodded as I spoke. "Indeed there would be no hope for mankind if mankind were mere apes as many 'scientists' suggest it is," said Helen, and than began to laugh. "But we are human beings. This puts a whole new dimension on things. No matter how deeply the mutilation of America has cut into the biological integrity that is designed to enhance the sexual, and thereby social, economic, and political intimacy in society, a mutilated society can still lift itself to a higher level of self-perception, where the biological factors for intimacy can be superseded with more powerful factors. So it doesn't really matter whether the biological mutilation is permanent or not. Our humanity doesn't end at the threshold of the biological factors. It extends beyond that threshold, where the spiritual dimension of our humanity unfolds. This doesn't mean that we should scrap sex altogether. It merely means that we need to develop mankind's spiritual dimension, that is richer and more secure than anything, that cannot be mutilated. To do this we only have to step into the realm of Love, the greatest source for intimacy there is, and also find our sex in its coming to light in countless forms of expression. Sex is no longer a tool then, or a means to an end, but stands as a symbol for something that biology merely hints at, and which we can embrace directly in a scientific manner and honor in celebration. This process and its celebration has the potential to shape the world. Even in a completely circumcised world, the sexual celebration remains a possibility. The vulva is still there, though it is increasingly blocked by the numerous machination conjured up by the empire's sewer rats. By uplifting sex to a level of spiritual celebration, that the rats cannot reach up to, the redevelopment of the Principle of the General Welfare on its original platform of intimacy, which biology merely builds a stage for, is still possible through the scientific process that builds the higher spiritual stage. So nothing is ultimately lost with the circumcision. We merely have to become more scientifically human to gain the higher levels of freedom. This means falling in Love with our amazingly wondrous and wide-ranging humanity. Most of that is located in the spiritual realm anyway, that science opens a pathway to, and in the realm of Love reflecting the qualities of the Universe and its underlying Intelligence."

"Are you saying that pursuing this path is what it means to become a world-historic person?" I interjected. "Are you saying that an uplifted sense of sex becomes the death knell of empire? Are you saying to sex, 'I love your promise and your power, and I love your assurance that the expression of the Principle of the General Welfare has not ended on this planet, but is just beginning to be raised up with effects never envisioned before?' If this is what we are saying when we speak of Love, Peter, which sex is just an aspect of, then the night of horrors has begun to be drawing to a close."

"Isn't this the promise that we find when we begin to understand universal history?" said Helen. "The more a person recognizes what mankind has accomplished from time to time, in pulling itself out of the private zoo of empire, by refusing to play the role of zoo animals or slaves, the more a person stands in awe of the unfolding spiritual journey that still lays before us all. Of course the stooges of empire scream that life isn't spiritual, but is material, and Love and Intelligence are irrelevant. They scream this, because without that kind of arrogant screaming, the zoo animals, or the slaves, would break out of their confinement. But do we heed the screaming? Many people do heed it. But don't we rather look at the achievements in history when society has claimed its humanity back? In a sense we are still fighting the effects of what the Pharaohs had begun, which are now strangling the whole world. But we have also discovered the historically proven resources to win our freedom back, by recognizing the Principle of the General Welfare as an aspect of Love, which is itself an aspect of the Principle of the Universe. If Love is not becoming manifest in a new renaissance of the Principle of the General Welfare, at least in some form, then our sense of Love is far too small to be counted. It's an empty shell then, a gong without a tone, a tale of dreams. That's a call then to go back to the drawing board, back to history."

"I guess this is the reason why my friend Erica was stuck, and I was despondent about it," I interjected. "She is a scientist, but she didn't know history. Neither did I. We didn't know what a historically motivated individual is, as you have defined it. You say that being in Love with our humanity opens up a frontier, but this is a demanding frontier. It demands corresponding action that rebuilds, what has been lost to slavery. Of course you are right. Without the motivation that brings the universal history of mankind into the sphere of Love, the stumbling blocks appear insurmountable. Without the larger dimension coming into view, our sense of Love tends to be too small. It tends to be too encumbered and impotent. I think this is why Erica was afraid to let the intimacy of her loving unfold fully. She was still playing the Pharaoh's game, but she does so voluntarily."

"I don't know where the motivation comes from that limits the natural intimacy between people," said Helen. "The Renaissance should have ended this trek to hell."

"Maybe Hobbes and the other philosophers like him have done this, who promoted such ideas," I said to Helen. "Hobbes proclaimed in essence that a human being is incapable of loving, and therefore the human being is his own worst enemy, so that the hand of authoritarian power must control the human being as a protection from itself. Hobbes suggested that the very notion of Love as a legitimate benign force in human affairs must be deemed a notion of treason and be punished accordingly, even with the death penalty if need be."

"I think Thomas Hobbes tried to break the last vestiges of the Golden Renaissance that society had still in their hearts, after an entire century of psychological warfare against it," said Helen. "Without Hobbes and other stooges of empire like him, the Thirty Years War might have been completely avoided. Instead it became the most brutal escapade of authoritarian madness prior to World War II. Thomas Hobbes, the Englishman who with his pen helped to destroy Europe, was of course honored for his achievement in the service of empire. He became the chosen 'philosopher of empire' and is still being honored as such, except by those who can see his real face as the king of all liars. 'In Lies We Trust!' was his hidden policy that enabled him to serve his masters well, and to voluntarily take on the role of a slave for it. For playing this role, even to earn the privilege to enter the palaces of his masters, Hobbes had to foreswear Love and the natural intimacy of human beings that sets the stage for the Principle of the General Welfare that the rulers of empire had feared like the plague. But I don't think that is where today's limiting of the natural intimacy in society originated. I think our searching for this takes us back much farther in time to the very early ages, where it might have grown out directly out of the Pharaohs' slavery system. The rulers of other empires might have recognized that the same effect that the Pharaohs had generated in the slave population with the rather brutal circumcision and infibulation, which stopped all intimacies, could be more easily achieved with the devices of religion. A religious dogma had become imposed that literally prevented people from being in Love with one another. In that religious dogma, Love was confined to the smallest possible form, the marriage of only two people. The doctrine also rendered a man and a woman as a form of property, governed by property laws, that define Love itself as subjected to these laws, so that its universal Principle almost fades out of sight. In this way the masters of religion have achieved the same effect that the Pharaohs had achieved by cutting away the foreskin of men and ripping out the clitoris of women together with scraping away the entire external vulva and sowing the large lips together with thorns. The inherent torture of this horrendous butchery is still unimaginable to me, Peter. In this sense religion may have offered a welcome compromise. Pious lifelong self-isolation was demanded from society by religion. And that had the same effect. In this way the masters of society created an effective alternative to sexual mutilation. In order to make the religiously created social mutilation of society enforceable, the rulers imposed the death penalty for transgressions. Hobbes didn't invent anything new, really. In some cases, the death penalty still applies, just as it did under Hobbes, when people fail to bow to dogma. And of course the religion continues to the present day. The dogma became tradition, called moral tradition. And where the dogma still rules, to the very day, men and woman are still being stoned to death for violating dogma. And of course, the dogma is still designed to protect empires. It almost seems that in order to protect the dogma, the circumcision was re-introduced, which creates willing slaves."

"Hasn't religion made matters worse?" I interjected. "Seeing that the circumcision takes away so much of a man's sexual sensitivity and thereby inhibits the natural cross-sexual intimacies, wouldn't the blocking of it open the door to homosexual practices. When the natural system is mutilated, so that the men's door to the women becomes closed, wouldn't this open the door wider between the men themselves, especially those who share the predicament? But religion slanders this 'emergency' response by so many men. Indeed, society itself calls them queer. Thus the victimized men in this trap, become doubly mutilated, often without realizing that they are in this trap. Honest religion would open the door towards healing the result of the first mutilation. Instead, religion has become an enemy of the victim and adds to the mutilation. No wonder many of the victims commit suicide."

"I think it is more complex than that, Peter," said Helen. "I think the human being is basically homosexual in nature. It is natural for us all to be at peace with ourselves as fully complete human beings, and to experience ourselves as being fully complete. We don't hate ourselves for that. We love our self-completeness for the riches it includes. That is our homosexuality. With that we can stand on the mountaintop and enrich one another in the celebration of the riches we have and are able to bring to one another. That's the natural outflow in the celebration of our completeness. The physical form of the celebration doesn't really matter, dos it, though the heterosexual form, is the most common form as it adds yet another dimension to the sense of self-completeness? If the female dimension weren't in your heart, Peter, why would you fall in love with it, as you do? Nevertheless, we are not merely male and female. We are spiritual beings with a vast range of still other spiritual qualities. These 'higher qualities' make us producers, creators, discoverers, and builders of civilizations. Here we stand not as male and female beside each other, but also with a third sex so to speak, that comes to light above the biological sphere, and the religions that would mutilate it. At the higher level of our third sex, nothing is mutable. The biologically mutilated can still reach that level of their third sex and embrace it fully, as we all must in the process of building our civilization. From this level we can also reach down and pull the lower levels up. We bring Science to insanity and create a sane world. The circumcision is insanity, Peter, and it can be left behind in the landscape of an ever brighter loving of ourselves and others and the truthful scientific platform."

"You are saying that religion was abused to isolate people, to prevent the development of intimacy and thus to keep the Principle of the General Welfare far out of sight?" I said quietly.

"For this objective the masters of religion have made the development of the Principle of Universal Love, a crime of God against humanity," said Helen. "People were taught to fear God, and to condemn Love in areas where it begins to unfold this principle."

"It appears that this old crime is still in effect," I said. "Are you saying that our modern society still lives in essentially the same environment that which the Pharaohs had pioneered for creating better slaves and controlling the slaves? It appears to me that in the case of the modern slavery, the enslaving environment goes deeper than what is visible at the surface. I suppose that this might be the reason why Erica couldn't celebrate her intimacy in Love, and ran away from it, when she found herself facing the deep barriers that she had learned to fear."

"What she couldn't deal with, is nothing more than a cleverly engineered factor that makes Hobbes look like an amateur in comparison," said Helen. "She couldn't deal with it, because what she

69

tried to deal with doesn't pertain to anything natural. It doesn't even exist as a factor in the complex domain. It is nothing more in real terms than a fog. This fog is currently pervading almost all cultures, turning societies into slave-like subjects. Some societies have added the circumcision, to intensify the fog, and to further blot out any chance for a developing intimacy that leads to the Principle of the General Welfare. It is because of this treachery that empire still rules the world, and that society bends to the will of its masters like a bunch of dancing slaves."

"Then the most valuable gift that Erica gave me is her honesty in illustrating how dense that fog really is that the whole world is now facing," I said to Helen. "If she couldn't cut through this fog as a scientist with two high academic degrees and being a woman who is engaged in studying Love, the fog must be incredibly dense. How then can anyone cut through it?"

"I would say that your friend Erica failed, because she does not yet see herself as a world-historic person," Helen interjected. "She doesn't see the deep black void that all insanity is, standing behind the fog. Nor does she recognize yet the sanity of Science. Science is sanity. Science focuses for us the light of Intelligence. Insanity is a black void in which nobody can really move."

"I think Erica has some inkling about what the Principle of the General Welfare is. Maybe she merely lacks the historic examples of mankind's power in fighting for its development. She seems to lack an understanding of the foundation that exists that she could build on. Nevertheless, her sense of the sanity of Science gave her a lot of power already. She has turned an experience of rape into a higher sense of loving."

"I see you are beginning to recognize what a world-historic person is," said Helen, and began to smile. "You gave a wonderful gift today, to help a person in great need by contributing a large sum for a violin that will give my friend his life back. But is your heart aching just the same to uplift all mankind? Is your sense of Love still relatively small and limited, or has it grown to be as wide as the world of Love really is? The question is: are you still cheating yourself?"

"Maybe I am still caught in the same trap with her," I said quietly. "But I'm also struggling to get out of it."

"Ah, then you want to fulfill the natural role of a human being, by moving deeper into Love and struggling to become a world-historic person with the power to lighten the world with the Principle of the General Welfare," said Helen.

"Maybe the transition has already begun without me knowing it," I said. "I remember coming across a literature table of the LaRouche organization at the Chicago airport. The organization was in a political mobilization drive to save mankind from the potential of a nuclear holocaust. A proposal was put forward to bring the great nations of the world together in a cooperative effort to create a missile defense system that would be ten times more powerful in intercepting an attack than the attacking system was at the time. The proposed system would be based on new physical principles, to meet this kind of requirement, and that would require a cooperative development effort of many nations. The proposal was logical, as this combined effort would be made for the common benefit of all mankind. And more than that, the vast development effort would establish a network of cooperative relationships between the feuding nations. The outcome would have guaranteed peace in a world standing at the precipice, because of the growing isolation of people and nations from one another. What the LaRouche people offered was a great proposal, for building an active peace in a time when the doomsday clock was standing at just minutes to midnight."

"So what happened to it?" Helen interjected.

"What do you think happened?" I said this with a wicked kind of smile. "The LaRouche people had a large display poster set up by their table, and the table was set up at the most prominent spot at the airport, where most of the foot traffic comes together. Thousands of people must have walked by their table in the morning, before I saw them. Let me tell you what happened. I came by there at around noon. I asked one of the fellows during my conversation with them, for the sake of interest, how much money they had collected this morning in support of their fight to save civilization against the threat of those 65,000 nuclear bombs that had been deployed around the world. Remember that the life of every person on the planet was in danger in this timeframe. The fellow I spoke with showed me the collection box. It contained a single five-dollar bill and a few coins. The entire donation added up to just over ten dollars. And that, Helen, was all that those thousands, who saw the poster, had deemed civilization to be worth, and their own existence with it. That's what happened. And that is why the proposal died."

"What you saw was not a normal society, Peter. You saw the face of a disconnected and isolated society," said Helen. "It would have been surprising if your experience had been any different, considering that America has been smothered under the mantle of the circumcision that has been thrown across America in the postwar period. By this single act the American society lost whatever sense of intimacy with one another, and with the nation, it might have had. I bet no one remembered the days when the Principle of the General Welfare still meant something. You experienced a tragedy. But you didn't answer my question, Peter. Are you a world-historic individual?"

"Well, I personally added a fifty to the collection can. Does this count for something?" I said to Helen in defending myself. "Maybe I should have stood behind the table with them and promoted an awareness of the Principle of the General Welfare. Maybe this would have been better."

"That would have been a more active form of involvement," said Helen, and nodded.

"I didn't do this; I regret to say. Maybe others did," I said. "Somehow the world survived by the efforts of those others, and continues to do so. Still, I think I didn't fail totally. I contributed something to the resources these people needed for them to raise the issue of universal defense, and become successful in their fight of changing the political landscape towards that. In fact, the landscape has changed after that, Helen. A gradual trend of nuclear disarmament began. The global nuclear stockpile has been reduced by 10,000 since those days. Of course I could have done more, like being actively with them on the front line. That's where I failed. And maybe, because of that failure, some of what should have been accomplished was not accomplished, for which the nuclear insanity now festers on in the background, enabling worse tragedies to happen, for which the world's children and their children may curse me one day in the future."

"So, Peter, all this considered, is it worth putting yourself on the line, when so much is at stake?" said Helen. "The more that people stay away from actively fighting for their humanity and their civilization, the more precarious the world becomes. Can we really afford that risk? In fact, can we even afford to sweep sex under the rug, as the religions would have us do, as something to be shunned, when so much is now at stake?"

I shook my head. "You said yourself that the religions have merely convoluted the process that the Pharaohs had started. The Pharaohs were more honest in their approach, though. The religions were used to hide the process. Of course we do this all the time in politics now at home," I said to Helen.

"Are you surprised, Peter?" said Helen. "When the goal is to enslave society to the masters of empire, all methods become acceptable."

"Oh yes, we do it by hook and by crook, and by stealth now," I said to her. "For example, if the empire-crowd that owns our President, wants something, they activate their stooge in chief, and the stooge sends a ten-page request of his master's demands to Congress to act on it. A ten-page request, however, tends to be too clear, so that the demands that come down from the empire wouldn't gather enough votes to have a chance to be accepted. When this happens, the request goes to committee. There it becomes convoluted into a 100-page document in which the real intention behind the bill becomes obscured with fancy formulations. If the resulting bill gets voted down in spite of all this, the stooge in chief will go to the Senate that will take the 100-page document and expand it into a 500-page document, interwoven with a bunch of trivial perks that the shallow-minded congress men would like to vote for. In this even deeper hidden form, the empire's bill goes back to Congress, wrapped up with glowing promises and pleas that it is all necessary. But which of the congressmen has the time and the capacity to read a 500-page document and understand the finely hidden points, and vote on it the next day? The result is that nobody reads the thing, and so it gets passed. In my book the entire process is one gigantic fraud. The congressmen that vote the bill up under those circumstances, commit treason by default. And of course society gets robbed in the process, and the masters of empire get fatter. That's how we make history in America now. We do it with treason. Stealth is treason."

"Are you surprised?" Helen interjected. "I would see it as a sign of a culturally defeated nation. The black mark is on the nation. You should see it as a warning. And what the stealth is all about is of the same category. Don't scream at the congressmen. The cause goes deeper and farther back, all the way to the Pharaohs."

"What this is all about is usually money, money conjured up as debt to the empire," I sad to Helen. "Of course we are a defeated nation, especially financially. The whole world is in that trap. No tax-paying society in the world really knows how big its debt really is, which is obviously so large that it can never be repaid. Nor is it intended to be repaid. The intention is to cause debt-bound servitude, and maintain it forever. Except that destroys the productive economy. So, the scheme can't possibly work. The whole pyramid of empire monetarism is bound to collapse. That's the horrid face of the so-called glory of the western world, my dear. It's a mess. Unfortunately, nobody pays any heed to the stinking mess behind the gilded front. I would say the whole world has been defeated, without exception."

"Isn't that what I said, Peter," said Helen.

"But what does it take to get this squared away?"

"That's what I meant when I said to you that it takes a world-historic person to see through the smokescreen before solutions can be found," said Helen. "You've got to understand the problem to find the solution. A world-historic person has no difficulties with that. Such a person, and there might be a few of them out there, would instantly see the connection between the currently ongoing scam, and what the Pharaohs had set up ages ago. So, I would say that the way in which you had reacted at the Chicago airport, doesn't measure up to the level of competence that would have been required then for the seriousness of the occasion."

"I did what I could, Helen."

"But were your actions any better in what you did, than the actions of those congressmen who routinely commit treason by default? Indeed, where your actions in Chicago significantly different than those of the thousands who walked by the LaRouche table without giving a damn? I would say that what you saw, and unwittingly became a part of, was not the response of a normal people. It was the response of a culturally defeated people. Maybe it should have been called treason too. That's where the actual tragedy lies that you encountered in Chicago. America is a defeated nation, Peter. You said this yourself. America has been culturally defeated. Don't tell me that America won World War II and saved the world. World War II was nothing in comparison to a cultural warfare attack. World War II only killed 50 million people, and when it was over Europe recovered and a decade later it was rebuilt. No nation was really defeated by that war. But how does one really destroy a nation? How does one defeat a society more completely than with the nuclear bomb? How does one defeat a nation so deeply that it can never recover, possibly for centuries? How does one do this? One does it culturally. And that is being done almost globally. The masters of empire who are greedy, mean, and insane do this with intention. The process of the inner destruction is already so far advanced, Peter, that even you have become too blind to recognize that it is happening."

"Are you saying that America has already been defeated that way?" I interjected. "I can't accept that?"

"When a nation is in mortal danger and doesn't give a damn to protect itself, that nation is a culturally defeated nation," said Helen. "It happens rarely in history. The last time this happened was in the 14th Century, and that was a mild case in comparison with what is happening today. Both the professor and I told you about the great Lombard banking-collapse in 1345. The Lombard banks had looted all of Europe and put Europe into an insane stranglehold of debt slavery. When the English king defaulted, and he wasn't the only one who couldn't pay the interest of the debt, the

75

entire debt-bound system collapsed. But this collapse didn't free Europe from its stranglehold. When the financial system collapsed, the economy collapsed with it. In this chaos all of Europe collapsed. Two years later the weakened population was hit with the black plague. The plague spread like wildfire. How do you think Europe recovered from the resulting disintegration of its civilization? Well, it took Europe a hundred years to recover. Before that happened, however, Europe lost a third of its population. The important thing now is; how did it recover? Europe recovered through cultural development. It recovered through the kind of cultural development that, for example, Dante Alighieri had already started sometime earlier in Italy. Long before the collapse occurred and brought the house down, Dante had warned the society of his time of the insanity in the financial system, and of the dire consequences that would result on this path. He was exiled for his outspoken opposition. He was banished for life from his beloved Florence. But Dante didn't capitulate. He started to build up a cultural foundation for the recovery of society, that was needed, whether the crash occurred or not. For this purpose, Dante traveled through the whole of Italy and 'collected' the most expressive, and most beautifully sounding dialects, and constructed with them a high level language that could express complex ideas, which then would bring all of Italy together on those ideas, as an intimate and culturally connected nation. He promoted his new language with his own poetry that carried the kind of developmental ideas for which such a high-level language was needed. This enormous task, which took a lifetime, laid the basis in part, for Europe's recovery after its economy disintegrated, which he had predicted long before it happened. In the recovery process, his high-level language became the foundation for the Golden Renaissance in Italy. The same kind of language development was happening all over Europe, as a means for cultural rebuilding, especially in England, in Spain, and in a few other places. As I said earlier, a profound widespread scientific development was also a part of the recovery process. This started with the rediscovery of Plato and his scientific method for making discoveries, which later became institutionalized, in the teaching order called the Brotherhood of the Common Life. Of course the scientific education also took time to mature, but it was an essential component for the cultural recovery of Europe. Scientific thinking is actually so vital in this context, that it is in fact a form of spiritual development."

I raised my hand to interrupt her.

"No Peter, let me finish," said Helen. "I know what I am talking about. Let me give you an example. I had a scientific experiment built for a friend of mine who taught science in an elementary school. I had a cycloid experiment designed for her that illustrated the Least Action Principle. The experiment illustrated that the shortest path between to points is not always the quickest. The experiment used two steel balls, both were released simultaneously, one to roll down a straight-line ramp, and the other to roll down the steep curve of a cycloid ramp. The two ramps came together at the end. Each time the experiment was run, the steel ball that rolled down the longer path of the cycloid ramp, came to the endpoint before the one that rolled down the straight-line path, that was shorter. This amazed the kids. Of course they wanted to explore why this happened. I, in turn, was amazed by their dynamic involvement. They were in competition with each other, in asking question. And, Peter, you should have seen their smiles and felt their excitement in the process of making discoveries. It gave them a sense of identity. They were all participating. The hands went up and up. Before I knew it, the hour that I had been given had passed. This was a great hour. One of the kids even wiped the blackboard for me. Of course this amazing happening wasn't at all to my credit. That it wasn't became apparent during the next hour. I had been asked to present the same experiment to another class of similar age, taught by a different teacher. This time the class was a dead scene. No hands were raised. No questions were asked. I was done in ten minutes. I asked a few questions to encourage a response, but nobody was willing to answer. Most surprising was the lack of connection in this class between the kids. The difference between the two classes was that the primary teacher of the first class was a seventy-year-old teacher, who had been grounded in classical science, who had evidently inspired the kids in the art of making fundamental discoveries, whereas the other teacher was a product of the new-age teaching. The first teacher's background in classical science had awakened a part of the kids' humanity, which in turn had forged a link between them."

"So you learned from the kids," I interjected.

"I did indeed, Peter. That day I began to discover how a renaissance is created. It was an amazing discovery. Whoever wants to destroy a nation, Peter, has to take these kinds of cultural aspects away that really create a nation. Taking that away is more destructive than war. And that is what the masters of empire have done to America, and likewise all over the world. That is what you have seen the end-result of in Chicago. The cultural destruction of America began with the erosion of education, of classical science, of the English language itself, by narrowing down their use. The cultural warfare then added to this the erosion of music, and the erosion of sex, into an 'entertainment' pursuit. And all of this happened in parallel, and is still happening. When this happens to an entire nation, and to the whole world, culture disappears, civilization ends, and nothing of substance remains in society to rebuild a nation with. There remains only an empty shell. That is the kind of war that has already defeated America. Without a profound culture, society looses its connection to one another, to its past, to its posterity, even to the future of mankind. The focus becomes narrowed down to nothing greater than ones isolated little self focused on the present moment. The rest falls out of sight as irrelevant. That's why nobody could give a dam at the Chicago airport. Who in such a defeated state would care, whether the nation be defended against an impending doom or not? That question literally had become irrelevant. That's the current outcome of the imperial project for cultural freedom, meaning freedom from culture. And this affects you, my friend, too. You said you were surprised by what you saw, but you didn't ask the question of what it takes to get out of the death stupor that you saw. I can tell you from history that in Europe it took the defeated society a hundred years of development to get itself out of its mess of a collapsed civilization and to rebuild what was lost. When the modern financial system disintegrates, which it will, because the current debt-load can never be repaid but eats up progressively all that is of value, then the sheer weight of the created debt will cause the entire system to self-collapse. It may take America and the world a hundred years or more to rebuild itself out of the resulting economic and cultural black hole. And this, Peter, will happen all across the world. What happened in Europe in the 14th Century, is now staged for the entire world. This time far more people will likely perish than merely a third of the population, because in the modern world everything is financially interconnected. When the financial system falls, nobody eats. If the collapse happens in winter, few will have heated houses. God only knows how many will freeze to death then, of those who don't starve to death first, or become victims of the 200 million handguns that society is carrying. And as I said, this collapse will be global, because the collapsing financial system is global, but the hardest hit will be America. The collapse is actually already ongoing, because the focus has long ago been shifted away from producing for one-another as a society, to stealing from one-another, and from cultural development to cultural decay and cultural rape. That's America's mark in this age. Also there might also be war in the near future. The war will likely be nuclear, biological, or radiological, as if war could make matters worse in an already collapsed society. It will likely take more than a hundred years this time, for society to recover from this kind of collapse. This means that mankind cannot afford to go that route. But who will cause a change in direction? Who will reverse the cultural defeat that has already gripped America so deeply that nobody cares to defend it? America is set in the direction of a defeated nation in which the defeat is far advanced. At the present stage it takes nothing less than a world-historic person to recognize the danger that America is in, and more so to develop the kind of aspirations of Love in society that restores culture, that develops intimacy in society, that develops science, literacy, even music, and develops a nobler sense of sex. All of these steps are needed to cause a cultural, and then an economic, recovery. Economic prosperity is a cultural thing, Peter. It is not a monetary thing. The production of goods is a cultural process. The foundation for this will not be restored, however, until society becomes world-historically oriented. That's the only way in which the scourge of empire can be vacated from this planet. Right now no one is interested. This shows how great a task lies now before us, Peter. Also the cultural restoration has to be achieved on every level, beginning with the Pharaoh's circumcision and its religious derivatives, extending from there all the way to the cultural mutilation that the western society has been increasingly subjected to in the postwar period. The reversal can be achieved, Peter, but the longer society remains asleep on the job, and its world-historic task is not taken up, the more revolutionary will the recovery have to become to avert total chaos. A culturally defeated nation is a collapsing nation. Right now the growing insanity is making the recovery increasingly more difficult. Society seems to be intent to wait until its house falls down over its head. The injuries sustained thereby will make the task of rebuilding more difficult and evermore dangerous. I for one would rather have us repair our house to prevent its collapse. Maybe I am too idealistic to fight for that. What do you think, Peter? Am I?"

"Who can be too idealistic in the crisis you described, which you say we are in?" I said in my dazzled amazement. "Compared with you, I am an idiot. My reactions in Chicago amounted to nothing, really. I can recognize this now. I am a traitor then."

"Don't say this," said Helen gently. "You are not a traitor, Peter. You were asleep. You are waking up. That's something to celebrate. What you did and didn't do when you were asleep is water gone under the bridge. The important question is, will you join these people's cultural restoration team today and lend a helping hand? Will you fight alongside with those who devote their life to the protection of mankind as an aspect of the Principle of the General Welfare? Doing that, is real living, Peter. You gave me three thousand marks for a violin to help a single man. Would you give fifty thousand for the survival of mankind if you had the money?"

I nodded quietly, but uncertainly. "Maybe I am still too much of a coward for that," I added.

"Ah, at least you are honest," said Helen and smiled. "That's a start. In this case you should awake yourself more completely to your native quality as a world-historic person, and step out of your dark house into the sunshine. History isn't just defined by what has happened in the past. History is made now. The more important part of it is how our unfolding sense of universal humanity shapes the present in order to determine the future. That is how we shape the flow of future history. If you are not concerned with mankind's future history, the best knowledge of the past has no meaning and your humanity remains an empty shell. The questions that you should ask yourself therefore each night, before you go to bed, are strikingly similar to what you had once asked yourself as a kid. You should ask yourself daily if our actions of the day have mattered to mankind? You should ask yourself if it was worthwhile for the world that you have lived in it. A positive answer would be good. It would be good for you, because then you would see your living as having a tangible value and a real immortality? This means that your evaluating yourself daily, must also include your asking if you see yourself actively as an immortal person? Most people don't consider this question. That is why the world remains just as poor as if its people had not lived at all, because they had contributed nothing of value to the wealth of its culture. I suspect that this is the reason why the world has become so incredibly poor and society has become so deeply defeated by the masters of empire. With this in mind, I personally keep asking myself what the purpose of living is, if it isn't for bringing out the colors of Love? This question brings to the forefront wonderful answers, and opens the door to actively making history. Shaping the world by acting from within the sphere of Love, is all that really counts in the end."

"Those thousands of people that I know must have passed by at the LaRouche table at the O'Hare airport that day, who couldn't give a penny towards saving civilization, were then essentially dead as human beings," I said. "As you said, they were already culturally defeated. It is really not surprising then that they didn't give a penny," I added quietly. "The dead won't give a penny. The dead have lost their will to live, and have buried their heart in a coffin."

Helen burst into laughter. "That's funny and tragic," she said. "I know a lot of those kinds of people too. But I'm not letting them sleep in peace in their coffin, I can tell you that. I make it too costly for them to sleep, because the outcome of their sleeping is too costly for us all. Also I would be cruel not to wake them. Most of human history, as least for the last five millennia, has been shaped by the slime molds of empire, that like a narcotic have put people to sleep in order that they become better slaves. It's cruel towards mankind to let this continue. In fact, it is a crime against humanity to sleep in this crisis, when the very future of mankind is at stake. My question is, are you willing to join me in waking people up from the slumber of their slavery, by helping them to discover their native life? Are you willing to do this as an active expression of the Principle of the General Welfare, which is an active aspect of their being in Love with their humanity and the common universal humanity of mankind? You will be able to recognize the spark of it when you are doing this, by the intensity of your own celebration of the wonders of our humanity. This path involves discovering Love. If you find great value in it, you invariably celebrate it by defending mankind and by organizing the general development of mankind as an aspect of being in Love in the widest sense possible. Also, if you celebrate the value of humanity in the truest sense as Love demands, you will thereby celebrate the doom of empire, because empire, like the fabled vampire, cannot exist in the sunshine. In the case of the unfolding light of universal Love, the sunshine unfolds in the form of the Principle of the General Welfare. For five thousand years the masters of the world have seen this principle on the horizon and seen it as a poison to their existence. Now it finally may be raised taller, and be brought home to become their doom. The unfolding of Love is on the horizon, Peter. Its dawn cannot forever be held back."

Helen stopped talking after saying this. She quietly resumed making the sandwiches. She sliced the olives in half, removing the stone. She sliced the pickles diagonally, and arranged everything on a clear glass platter, with four pickled onions placed at the center.

"May I touch your hair?" I said quietly, while she made the final arrangements.

She turned to me and smiled. "You may touch anything you are in Love with about me, because your loving is honest."

"Honest?" I repeated.

"Of course, honest," she affirmed. "If loving is lustful, that's dishonest, because it means rape. In that case, you wouldn't have asked, but forged ahead. But you couldn't have done that, because you are a world historic person. And so you have asked. You have asked with a respect for sovereignty in year heart, and you have asked also for the sheer joy of it. That's obvious. This is honest, Peter, and it will make us both richer. Intimacy is one of the pillars of civilization, if not the central pillar, but it is only possible in celebration. When you enter the temple for celebration, then you recognize that being honest means that you are in Love with me, and with yourself, primarily as a human being. No lust enters there. Anything else would be dishonest."

"I see you first and foremost as both a human being and a woman," I interjected. "Forget about all the other roles people play, hierarchical roles, like brother, sister, lover, wife. We are much more closely related as human beings. Does that count?"

"Of course it counts. That's all what counts," said Helen. "Every vertical relationship adds a touch of isolation. Hierarchical relationships create a vertical world. They isolate people. They always have. But as human beings we stand side by side as equals. Can you think of a closer relationship than that? Touching me on that platform is honest, because that platform is true."

"Is this the zero-distance platform of the lateral world where Love is the Light of Life?" I said and grinned.

She said that it was.

In this environment her hair felt beautiful to touch, as beautiful as it looked, smooth, in flowing lines. There was a great sense of joy unfolding from this growing intimacy.

I asked her moments later, "What did you mean, when you said, for the sheer joy of it? Did you mean the joy that makes the very air sparkle?"

She didn't answer. She couldn't. I prevented the answer with a kiss. For a brief moment I even dared to touch her breasts, but within seconds I pulled my hands back and let them slide away along her side, down to her skirt. It seemed all too daring. "Popular opinion says that one mustn't touch a woman if one is a man and is not married to her," I said in a small voice.

"That's slavery, Peter," she replied. "Don't be a slave to that opinion. That's Pharaoh speaking, disguised as morality, but with the original effect. Respond to Truth instead of to Pharaoh. Be truthful. Respond to Love. Respond to your humanity, the humanity that we all share."

She turned around with a smile. "The clasp for my skirt is at the back," she said, and began to grin. "If it is too restrictive, take it off. Take the panties off, too." She said that there is the same beauty in Life and in Love, as there is in Truth. "Those are the constituents of our being."

She kissed me briefly. She took hold of the plate of sandwiches and complements and carried them into the good room. I carried the tea and the cups.

As it turned out her skirt wasn't too restrictive. Nevertheless, she excused herself after a few moments and changed into something "more appropriate," as she put it. She should have called it something "more exciting." It certainly was that. She wore a full-length, feather light dressing gown when she returned. It was almost transparent. Being with her became a sexual delight. There was a beauty in these moments of a growing intimacy in which there wasn't the slightest haste. It was born by a promise that felt secure. Indeed, her earlier promise was already coming true, when she said, "You can touch anything you are in Love with about me.'

I commented on what a delightful feast this had become; a feast enriched with sex, olives, and smiles.

"That spells out SOS," she said and burst out laughing.

"Yes, it has become an SOS type of a day for both of us," I said and joined her laughter.

"I think we both needed to be rescued," she added.

I agreed. Still, I shook my head in disbelief, as she stood before me like a beautiful white angel. I shook my head and smiled.

"Enjoy yourself Peter, embrace the world," was her reply, "the principle of Love is universal. It cannot be limited nor be made conditional. If you are in Love with yourself, you simply are in Love with all. There is no isolation rational in this sphere, since we all share the same humanity. I don't exist apart from it as someone different. That is the truth. That's what Love acknowledges. That's what freedom is all about. Nicholas of Cusa, a dear friend of mine, one of the creators of the Renaissance, championed the idea of natural and universal freedom and unity."

"Heh, Cusa has lived 600 years ago," I reminded her.

"Of course he has," but he is still my friend. "I feel close to him, because of what he represents."

I enjoyed listening to Helen. She was right about so many things. Certainly she was right about me. I had not known before I met her, what Love is. I had never seen it as an universal impetus that needs to be understood in its universal context, or else it can't be understood at all. Helen had opened up a whole New World to me with vast new implications that I now had to face. But did I understand any of it?

Probably not. Obviously, that was the reason why I had let my hands fall away from her breast.

At one point in our conversation, with our drinks and snacks in hand, Helen showed me the rest of the apartment. The apartment had a balcony, accessible through the kitchen. It offered a view of a small park as I could make out. The bathroom, however, was tiny, with barely enough room for a tub and a small counter. There was a blue glowing glass sculpture at the end of the counter. The single bedroom in the apartment was large in comparison. The bedroom furniture was modern, painted white. Her bed was huge, king sized, if not bigger. A floor-to-ceiling mirror graced one wall.

Shortly after we entered the bedroom Helen turned the main lights off. She shed her gown and crawled into bed. "Come, Peter," she said gently.

My reaction must have seemed like that of an idiot. I just stood there, and couldn't move. I wanted to respond. I wanted this above anything I could think of, just to be with her, but I couldn't move.

"Do I make you feel uncomfortable?" she asked. "But why should you feel that way? How many times a week do you go to bed with your wife? Every night, usually. Am I right? So, why not now? Am I not a woman, just like your wife is? Or am I a lesser woman?"

"No Helen, you are a great woman and a great person. You are a dream to be with."

"Ah, that's not it then," she said and smiled. "Are you saying that you have never had any close, intimate moments of sexual sharing with a woman before in your entire life? Is that why you are hesitant?"

"Of course I have had sexual intimacies with a woman before, on countless occasions, with my wife," I answered.

I remember that I had begun to laugh as I said this. I had sounded so stupid, so silly. It was obvious what this was leading towards, but it was also rather beautiful what was unfolding, because it brought to light what the principle of truthfulness with oneself really is. What was unfolding came to light as something far greater than I had thought it would be. I could think of no principle to support the narrow concept that I had clung to for so long. Still, I had let the old train of thinking continue that night in order to discover what else I had not discovered before.

"Then you are saying to me that I am not as much a human being as your wife is?" Helen continued our conversation, which she may have recognized had become a game, but one that needed to be played out to the logical end, to clear the air.

"No, Helen, you are a beautiful human being and a beautiful woman all at the same time," I replied in my defense, "who could ask for anything more?"

"Tell me then, Peter, what prevents you from being truthful with yourself, and with me? Would you not love to be with me in bed, at this very minute?"

"I would love nothing better," I answered. "It would be the greatest joy. I have dreamed about a situation like this, for so long, like you wouldn't believe, and here I stand and find it difficult to take that one last simple step. I am an idiot, right? I am untruthful with myself and with you. Do you want me to tell you why? The reason is that we have all been taught for centuries to be untruthful with ourselves and with one-another. That's why I can't move. It's anchored in time!"

Helen began to laugh. "If you could only hear yourself! But what is time? That's a tough one to break, Peter, isn't it?" She continued gently. "It is the toughest challenge that I have encountered. It prevents us from accepting our universal humanity. Living as slaves to time and tradition has become a deadly failure in civilization, Peter. What the Pharaohs created also became a tradition. Do you know what the social name for the infibulation of women is? The name is tradition! Do we need to honor tradition? Millions of women are mutilated for the sake of tradition every year. Or do we need to honor Truth? That is my imperative."

"We recognize the principle of the universality that supports our unity as human beings, in which we are all one," I said to her.

"Oh yes, we even say we understand it," said Helen. "But do we understand it? We have proof of it, as your dream illustrates, and still we deny ourselves, and doubt what our scientific mind has already acknowledged as Truth. What a paradox! We have lived like that for a very long time, Peter."

"The Truth is," I replied to her, and the laughter faded as I said this, "you are as much a star in the heavens of our humanity, as a woman, as my wife is as a woman, or any other woman I have ever met. At this level we are truly all one. We reflect and share a common humanity. As you say, there is no difference at the leading edge."

"I didn't say, there is no difference," Helen replied immediately. "You said this. But I can tell you this; we are both more profoundly and deeply married to each other, you and I, as human beings, than the marriage division isolates us that you are putting so much emphasis on. Our universal marriage as human beings is rooted in Truth. It is a part of the reality of our being. What isolates us, in comparison with that, is artificial."

I was stunned. I didn't know what to reply. I had said almost the same thing to Erica earlier, but that had been theoretically spoken then. Helen suggested that I be honest with myself now and acknowledge what the Truth is that I had long recognized to be true. This became a challenge I hadn't expected, or hadn't prepared myself for.

"I like to agree with you that you are right," I said in reply. "We are all married to each other as human beings. We are this by the countless wonders that we share as members of the human family. That's what we find reflected in our common humanity. I suppose you are right also that this natural marriage goes deeper, and is more profound, than anything we have come up with to artificially symbolize the principle that unites us. I suppose the truth is, that we are brothers and sisters then, of the family of man, and should treat each other that way."

I began to laugh as I said this. It seemed silly now to consider how badly we respond to what is obviously true. "Isn't it silly," I said to her, "that we find it so hard to accept what is so evidently anchored in the Truth? Isn't is silly that we are more inclined to see each other as enemies, and treat each other that way, than to be in Love with each other for what we all share? Isn't it silly of us that we do all of this in the name of some superimposed civil arrangement that we have invented in the name of making our life richer, but which denies the very reality that it aims to build on? Indeed, why should we deny the riches of our humanity that unite us, for something that is artificial? Shouldn't it be the other way around? Shouldn't the artificial be elevated to reflect the reality of our being, by our commitment to embrace ever more of the wondrous reality by which we are all united as human beings?"

Helen didn't respond with laughter this time. Her face lit up with something brighter than a smile. "This is what I mean, Peter, and it starts here. I can also tell you this," she added, "there are very few people who stood at this spot where you stand right now, who have made this kind of profound statement and presented it so clearly. This means that my invitation still stands for you to be truthful with yourself, and with me, and the whole of humanity, and to acknowledge what you know to be true."

As she said this, she pulled the sheets back on the side of the bed where I stood. But immediately she reversed the process, got out of bed, and put her gown back on. "The air is still too heavy," she said. "More healing is needed. You face a barrier that you don't even know of. Except this cannot be dealt with in bed."

Without another explanation she went into the kitchen and refilled the kettle. She placed it on the stove, silently.

"What barrier?" I said cautiously. "Another tradition?"

"It's a tradition that was never understood, Peter," she said and brought a bag of cookies to the table. She motioned me to join her there. "Would you like one?" she said.

"Does the tradition have a name?" I asked, as I reached for the cookie bag.